The Wilderness
of God

The Wilderness of God

ANDREW LOUTH

Let the wilderness and the dry-lands exult,
let the wasteland rejoice and bloom,
let it bring forth flowers like the jonquil,
let it rejoice and sing for joy.

Isa. 35:1–2

Darton, Longman and Todd
London

First published in 1991 by
Darton, Longman and Todd Ltd
89 Lillie Road, London SW6 1UD

British Library Cataloguing in Publication Data
Louth, Andrew
  The wilderness of God.
  1. Christianity. Special subjects. Deserts
  I. Title
  261.55

ISBN 0–232–51876–9

Phototypeset by
Input Typesetting Ltd, London SW19 8DR
Printed and bound in Great Britain by
Courier International Ltd, Tiptree, Essex

To the Sisters of
the Community of St Clare
at Freeland

Contents

Preface

The idea for this book was suggested by Lesley Riddle, while
she was Editorial Director at Darton, Longman and Todd:
without the impetus of her suggestion it would never have
been written. I owe a debt of gratitude to many other people,
too many to mention. It is dedicated to the Sisters of the
Community of St Clare, in gratitude for their 'oasis' at Freeland.

Darlington   ANDREW LOUTH
Feast of the Conception by the Righteous
Anna of the Most Holy Mother of God, 1990

Acknowledgements

Almost all the Scripture quotations in this publication are from the Revised Standard Version of the Bible, copyright 1946, 1952, 1971 by the Division of Christian Education of the National Council of the Churches of Christ in the USA. The quotations from *Collected Plays* and *Collected Poems 1906–1962* by T. S. Eliot are made by permission of Faber and Faber Ltd.

Introduction

The desert has a special place in the Christian tradition –
and in those traditions that it has built on or made its own,
especially the Hebrew tradition. It is a place of beginning, a
place where the human is refined and God revealed. The
burning bush, which called Moses aside and gave him the
task of leading the people of Israel out from slavery under
Pharoah, was in a desert: he led the Israelites out into the
desert, and there they remained until a generation had passed,
nomadic wanderers in the desert, until the time of testing and
preparation was completed and they were ready to enter the
Promised Land. John the Baptist, the prophet who pro-
claimed the advent of the Messiah, lived in the desert; Jesus
was tested in the desert; Paul, after his conversion, retired
into the Arabian desert (maybe for years) to prepare himself
for his mission to the Mediterranean world. As the Church
lost its first youth and in the fourth century began to become
an accepted part of Roman society, many Christians – thousands, or even tens of thousands of them – went out into the
desert, first to the Egyptian desert, later to the desert south
of Palestine and the steppe beyond Syria, to find a purer,
more austere, less compromised form of Christianity. The
great mountains of biblical revelation are all in the desert:
Horeb (also called Sinai), in the shadow of which Moses saw
the burning bush, and where Moses received the Law;
Carmel, where God vindicated the faith of the prophet Elijah;
Tabor, the Mount of the Transfiguration. The journey into
the desert, the ascent of the mountain in the desert: these are
powerful symbols of the experience exacted by God of those
who seek him. Even to go on a pilgrimage to the Holy Land

1

is to find oneself in a country invaded by the desert, which
stretches south of the holy places towards Egypt in all its
barren austerity.

The desert has appealed – still appeals – as a reality:
the Egyptian desert is a barren wilderness; the Cistercian
monasteries of the twelfth century were built in places remote
from civilization; the Russian forest, the *taiga*, virgin, dangerous and impenetrable, became the Russian 'desert'; Charles
de Foucauld lived in the Sahara desert of North Africa. It is
also a symbol, what it symbolizes is suggested by its very
name: barren desolation in the English *desert*, the German
Wüste, the Russian *pustynia*; or more precisely, solitude, in the
Greek *erēmia* (which also suggests the similar sounding *ēremia*,
stillness), and the Latin *solitudo*. It thus suggests a state of
extreme simplicity, stripped of anything unnecessary, even
the pleasures (and cares) of civilized, or cultured, life, and
especially the comfort and distraction of society, of other
people. It is an ideal that is both firmly rooted in Christian
tradition and yet an ideal that seems to conflict sharply with
much that is central to Christianity, especially its emphasis
on love of one's neighbour: 'Whose feet will you wash?' Basil
tartly asked enthusiasts for the solitary life. It has been paradoxical in its fruits: classical learning and culture were preserved by those very monks whose ideal spurned such culture:
Catullus survives in a single manuscript copied by a medieval
monk.

Even what life in the desert is like is conceived of ambiva-
lently. Many monastic writers speak of the desert, whether
the literal desert or the conditions of the desert the monk
finds in his cell, as a place not just of solitude (*erēmia*), but of
stillness (*ēremia*) or quietness (*hēsychia*): a stillness and quietness that makes it possible for the mind to withdraw from the
distraction of the world and its cares and devote itself to
contemplation of God. Other monastic writers speak of the
desert as a place of struggle, of hand-to-hand combat with
demons, of temptations, inflamed imagination, and for those
successful in this combat, of pride. In their writings (a notable
early example is St Athanasius' *Life of St Antony*) the desert
seems to be a noisy, clamorous place, worse than the world,
not a place of quiet or stillness at all.

The imagery of the desert can appeal in very different ways. In the lines (her own, despite the 'anon.') with which Rose Macaulay prefaced her novel *The World my Wilderness*:

> The world my wilderness, its cares my home,
> Its weedy wastes the garden where I roam,
> Its chasm'd cliffs my castle and my tomb . . .

the wilderness is a place of delight, of nostalgia, though with a sombre tincture. For Thomas Hardy, his wilderness, Egdon Heath, was a place that impressed sensitive men and women with a sense of melancholy, or more precisely pessimistic, brooding:

> It was at present a place perfectly accordant with man's nature – neither ghastly, hateful, nor ugly: neither commonplace, unmeaning, nor tame; but like a man, slighted and enduring; and withal singularly colossal and mysterious in its swarthy monotony. As with some persons who have long lived apart, solitude seemed to look out of its countenance. It had a lonely face, suggesting tragical possibilities . . . The untameable, Ishmaelitish thing that Egdon now was it always had been. Civilization was its enemy; and ever since the beginning of vegetation its soil had worn the same antique, brown dress, the natural and invariable garment of the particular formation.

Someone of genuinely melancholy demeanour, Jaques in *As You Like It*, is finally drawn to the desert. His melancholy, to begin with, protects him from the easy delight in the Forest of Arden (or Ardennes), affected by the exiled Duke:

> Are not these woods
> More free from peril than the envious court?
> Here feel we but the penalty of Adam,
> The seasons' difference; as, the icy fang
> And churlish chidings of the winter's wind,
> Which, when it bites and blows upon my body,
> Even till I shrink with cold, I smile and say
> 'This is no flattery: these are counsellors

That feelingly persuade me what I am.'
Sweet are the uses of adversity . . .

Here there is the contrast, which runs through the play like
an undercurrent, between civilization – two-faced, deceitful
and deceiving – and the desert, as the forest is often called,
where disguises only reveal truth, and the obliqueness of
civilized manners is short-circuited. At the end of the play
the usurping Duke Frederick comes to the forest to put an
end to his brother, the usurped Duke, but

> . . . to the skirts of this wild wood he came,
> Where, meeting with an old religious man,
> After some question with him, was converted
> Both from his enterprise and from the world.

All rejoice at the restoration of their fortunes, except Jaques,
who announces that he will stay in the forest and join up
with the now converted Duke Frederick, living in the 'abandon'd cave' of the now restored Duke:

> out of these convertites,
> There is much matter to be heard and learn'd.

What Jaques is to learn from those 'convertites' is not
divulged. That is not simply because it is 'another story', but
also because what those who have been drawn to the desert
have to teach is no simple 'message' but rather something
that is inseparable from their lives. Hence the most obvious
feature of this book: it is a study of various people who have
been drawn to the desert. It begins with probably the most
famous 'desert saint' of the twentieth century: Charles de
Foucauld, first drawn to the desert as a young soldier – rather
like Lawrence of Arabia – by its glamour, who later found in
the desert the uncompromising spirituality that he craved,
which has had such an appeal to so many in this century.
But alongside Charles de Foucauld, we find another 'desert
father', his confessor and spiritual director, the Abbé Huvelin.
His desert was no literal desert of sand – he lived all his life
in Paris – but an inner desert of mental anguish which,

however, bore remarkable fruit in his work of spiritual direction. This first chapter, then, introduces something of the diversity of the desert ideal, both external and interior, both a place that allures and a state of desolation. We then look at the sources of the desert tradition in Christian spirituality: in the Scriptures, and in the experience of the desert in the Near East, first in Egypt, later in Palestine and Syria, in the fourth and immediately succeeding centuries. What follows is no systematic survey of the desert tradition in Christian spirituality – that can be found elsewhere* – but a series of studies of distinct appropriations of that tradition, ending by coming full circle into the twentieth century with a study of the value T. S. Eliot placed on that tradition and how it influenced his poetic vision. In all its forms, it is a tradition that goes to the very limits of what is humanly possible and there 'somewhere on the other side of despair' discerns 'the city that has foundations, whose builder and maker is God'.

*For a systematic account of the development of the various forms of the desert life in the Christian tradition, see Peter F. Anson, *The Call of the Desert* (London, 1964; repr. with new introd., 1973.)

1

Charles de Foucauld and the Abbé Huvelin

On 1 December 1916, in the North African desert, Charles de Foucauld – Charles de Jésus, as he had called himself for a long time – was shot dead by one of the Tuaregs, the native people amongst whom he had been living as a priest since 1909. He died in the desert, the desert that had attracted him for most of his life. First it had attracted him as the unknown, undiscovered country he had explored as a young French cavalry officer; finally it had attracted him as a place where he could live out most perfectly that 'life hid with Christ in God' (Col. 3:3), a place deprived of the recognized presence of Christ, where, as a priest, he could say mass, effect the real presence of Christ, and live a life of adoration of the One who so empties himself as to encounter men and women in the bread and wine of the Eucharist. The desert that attracted the bored young soldier, and the desert that lured the monk from the austerities of la Trappe, the priest from the Holy Land, was the same desert: the demands it made on the soldier that nothing else could satisfy were much the same demands that it made on the monk and the priest. Though the young soldier had lost his faith and explored the desert for the thrill and the danger, and the monk and the priest felt his obedience to Christ calling him out to the desert, both weary unbelief and strenuous faith found that the desert met their extreme needs. When after his conversion Charles de Foucauld lived for some years the life of a Cistercian of the Strict Observance (a Trappist), and lived that life with the added austerities of the small, make-shift priory at Akbès in Syria, the memories of his journeys of exploration in Morocco reminded him that monastic poverty had not the austerity he craved: he wrote to his spiritual director, the Abbé Huvelin, 'you hope that I have poverty enough – No; we are poor compared with the rich, but not poor as our Lord was, not poor as I was in Morocco, not poor as St Francis.'[1]

Charles de Foucauld was born into a wealthy and noble French family on 15 September 1858. His parents died when he was five, and he and his sister were brought up by their grandparents. He was brought up devoutly, but lost his faith in his teens, chose the career of a soldier (as an easy option), and graduated from the Ecole de Saint-Cyr. He lived gaily as a young officer. His regiment, the Fourth Hussars, was sent to Algeria in 1880 and in 1881 he was engaged in the suppression of an insurrection there. His experience of Africa made him want to study it, and explore it, and the following year he set out on a journey of exploration of Morocco, which he described in his book, *Reconnaissance au Maroc*.[2] The danger – he travelled disguised as a Jewish rabbi with his Jewish guide, Mordechai – the extreme austerity, and the strangeness all excited him: the work of exploration was valuable in itself, his researches contributed importantly to knowledge of the geography of Morocco. When he finally returned to Paris in 1886 to put together the fruits of his travels, he was much celebrated, and looked forward to further voyages of exploration. The appeal of strange countries might have made of him yet one more Victorian traveller and explorer. But it seems – something scarcely surprising – that his long, solitary days of travel, and his experience of the religious culture of Islam, with its regular calls to prayer and its sense of the reality of God, had provoked a crisis in the soul of Charles de Foucauld. He felt a sense of the oddness of a society, if not secular, at least unconvinced of the reality of God, and the strangeness of his fitting in so naturally with such a society. In Paris too, through his contact with his aunt, Mme Moitessier, and her daughters – to one of whom, Marie, later Mme de Bondy, he became, and was to remain, very attached – he came to know people whose Christian faith was deep and real. Through them he encountered the curate of St-Augustin, the Abbé Huvelin, and through him there came his conversion. Early one morning towards the end of October 1886 Charles de Foucauld went up to the Abbé Huvelin's confessional and, without kneeling down, said, 'Monsieur l'Abbé, I do not have the faith; I have come to ask you to instruct me.' Huvelin looked at him and replied, 'Kneel down, make your confession to God: you will believe.' 'But I have not come for that.' 'Make your confession.' So Charles de Foucauld knelt and made his confession. When he had given absolution Huvelin asked him if he were fasting, and learning that he was, told him to go and make his communion – a communion that Charles de Foucauld regarded as his 'second first communion'.[3]

It was some months before Charles de Foucauld saw what the consequences of his conversion were to be. Soon, however, he realized that he must dedicate himself to God totally, as a monk or a friar. Huvelin counselled delay. In 1888/9, he made a pilgrimage to the Holy Land – to Jerusalem, Bethlehem, Nazareth – and then spent periods with various religious communities: with the Benedictines at Solesmes (Easter 1889), with the Cistercians of the Strict Observance at the Grand'-Trappe, with the Trappists again at Notre-Dame-des-Neiges, with the Jesuits at Clamart. He chose the Trappists and in January 1890 he joined the Abbey of Notre-Dame-des-Neiges, as a novice, on the understanding that he would complete his noviciate and become a monk at the priory in Akbès in Syria, a daughter-house of Notre-Dame-des-Neiges. The viscount Charles de Foucauld became Brother Marie-Albéric. In June he left France for Syria. He felt deeply his separation from his sister and his cousin, Marie: he was not giving up something that mattered little.

But la Trappe was not for him. He completed his noviciate and his period in simple vows, but traditional monasticism was too secure, too removed from the 'naked following of the naked Christ' that he sought. Or so it seemed to him. When he finally left the order in 1897, one of his fellow monks wrote that

he is the perfect image of our nobility of the nineteenth century, brave, generous in blood and money, saintly as is sometimes the case, but incapable of continued obedience and of discipline under a leader; he could become a saint, I hope he will, but in charge, not under obedience. He has made, I see, sacrifices too great and too fine for God to allow him to go astray; that, in my opinion, is the sole serious guarantee on the extraordinary way he is following[4]

though there was no actual breach of obedience in the way Charles de Foucauld left la Trappe; on the contrary, he was prepared to accede to any demands, even two years study in Rome in preparation for the priesthood (something, in the event, not demanded of him).[5]

On Huvelin's advice, Charles de Foucauld returned to the Holy Land, where he lived for the next three years, mainly at Nazareth, though for a short time at Jerusalem. He attached himself to a convent of Poor Clares (the second order of the Franciscans, a contemplative order for women) and became their sacristan, living in what was nothing more than a garden hut (he refused to live in the gardener's cottage the abbess offered him), looking after the chapel, fetching the nuns' post and doing other little errands. There he followed his own austere routine, more to his taste than that of la Trappe. He rose early and prayed until the time of the Angelus, then he went to the Franciscan convent and the grotto there, said to be part of the house the Holy Family had lived in, where he prayed the rosary and heard the masses said there; at six o'clock he went to the sisters, prepared the chapel for mass, and then served at the mass which was said at seven o'clock; then he swept the chapel (on Saturdays), on Thursdays and Sundays went to collect the post, and spent the day in various small tasks; at five in the evening he made ready for benediction and remained in the chapel afterwards, praying, until 7.30; he then went back to his 'hermitage' where he read until nine; finally, compline and bed. All the time he spent alone; he read by himself during meals, and broke up the day by half an hour of prayer at 10.30 and another half an hour at three – the time of the offices.[6] He describes all this in a letter that ends:

The more one gives to the good God, the more he gives back: I believed I had given all in leaving the world and entering la Trappe, I received more than I had given . . . Once again I have believed I have given all in leaving la

9

Trappe: I have been filled, filled beyond measure . . . I am infinitely joyful in being poor, dressed as a worker, a domestic servant, in that low condition which was that of Jesus our Lord, and as a crowning piece of exceptional grace, to be all that at Nazareth.[7]

He had found, it seemed, his way of imitating Christ, by sharing the poverty Jesus had known at Nazareth. In his extreme and literal desire to share that 'low condition which was that of Jesus our Lord' one hears an echo of one of the sayings of his spiritual director: 'Our Lord has taken the last place in such a way, that no one has ever been able to rob Him of it.'[8]

The shape of Charles de Foucauld's way begins to emerge: on the one hand, conditions of life, clothing, shelter, food, no better than that of the poorest; on the other hand, a life of prayer, not prayers, not devotions, but prayer, a state of being close to God, of being in his presence. And these two sides converge in his living a life close to that of the incarnate Son of God, in his poverty and ordinariness, and his sense of immediacy with God. Like St Francis, his way is the way of an imitation of Christ; and of that imitation, Nazareth is the symbol. As Huvelin put it in a letter to him at Nazareth: 'Bury yourself with our Lord, lost, unknown. It is your vocation.'[9] We can see, too, in what way the desert is becoming a symbol of Charles de Foucauld's vocation: the desert as a place of solitude, of hiddenness, a place of being alone with God in prayer. It is a place of presence: the purifying presence to oneself of solitude, and the still more purifying presence of God. Charles de Foucauld's sense of the presence of God among us found expression in his devotion to the Sacred Heart, and to the Eucharistic Presence as the presence of God's love amongst us. His favourite form of prayer comes to be adoration of the Reserved Sacrament. All this impresses itself on Foucauld in the Holy Land, in Nazareth, as he lived a life of prayer stripped even of the sparse props provided by the monastic tradition of la Trappe.

In Nazareth also Charles de Foucauld devoted himself to the study of theology, and found that this, too, deepened his life of prayer. Something that did not surprise Huvelin (with whom he kept in frequent contact by letter):

> I am not astonished that theology contributes at present to your recollection, to your prayer. It is quite simple. All that our Lord has done for us, He has done by love, and everything leads to making us love Him. Your mind was quite stiff; as it loosens, it is opened, it expands, it becomes gentle.[10]

This relaxed, gentler, more sensitive mind (or spirit – *esprit*) is thus able to grow. In two ways most strikingly. First, as he meditated day by day on the mysteries of the rosary in that place where he believed the voices of Mary, Joseph and Jesus had echoed, and amongst things that had known the touch of the eyes and hands of the incarnate Son of God, it was the mystery of the *Visitation* that came to assume for him special significance: the mystery of the visit made by the pregnant virgin Mary to her cousin Elizabeth, also miraculously pregnant with John the Baptist. The combination of presence – no presence more intimate than that of a child in his mother's womb – with her attention and care for another: Mary blessing another with the blessing of the presence of God in her womb – this was the mystery of the Visitation, and this became a symbol for Charles de Foucauld of his vocation.[11] But secondly the realization that though his life might be that of a hermit, being a hermit was not his vocation, or at least did not exhaust his vocation. Huvelin tried to dissuade Foucauld from thinking of founding an order, fearing no doubt the extremes of austerity of any rule Charles de Foucauld might compose. But from his time in Nazareth Foucauld ceased to think of himself as a hermit, and rather thought of himself as 'Charles de Jésus', one of the 'Little Brothers of the Sacred Heart of Jesus'.[12] During his own lifetime he only found one companion, and he did not last long: the austerity of brother Charles was too much for him (brother Michael eventually became a Carthusian). But since his death the inspiration of his life has led to the foundation of the Little Brothers and Sisters of Jesus[13] – small communities inspired by Charles de Foucauld's spirituality of poverty and adoration.

After three years he left the Holy Land and returned to France where he was ordained priest on 9 June 1901. There was thought of returning to the Holy Land, but instead he set out for another desert, another part of the desert of North Africa that had first attracted him. He went out to Algeria, where he spent the rest of his life, at oases in the desert, ministering to the French troops stationed out there, and living a life as poor and simple as the Berber tribes amongst whom he lived. First at Beni-Abbès and finally at Tamanrasset, he sought to establish his new kind of religious order in the Sahara desert.

The life he lived in the desert was much the same as that he had lived at Nazareth, except that his work included great labours on the language of the Tuaregs, the tribe amongst whom he lived, compiling a dictionary, collecting Tuareg poems, and even writing in the language himself. He became a formidable expert in an almost forgotten language. But the main structure of his life was as before: rising very early, spending long hours in prayer, eating very frugally, living in conditions of extreme simplicity. The difference now was his daily celebration of mass (when he could find someone to serve for him, until on the last day of 1908 he heard that papal permission had been given him to celebrate mass on his own)[14] – saying mass where mass had never been said before, making Christ sacramentally present where his sacramental presence had never been known before.

What was the point? To make Christ present sacramentally where he had never been before, to adore the incarnate presence of God, the Blessed Sacrament, where such adoration had never been known before. It was a missionary task, but a missionary task with a difference: he was there for the sake of souls that did not know Christ, but he had no notion of any crude conversions (in fact he made no converts at all). There is, to be sure, an uneasy ambiguity about Charles de Foucauld's understanding of his role in French North Africa. He speaks of his researches in Tuareg as a way of making the language a language the nomadic tribes can continue to use as civilization advances instead of taking up Arabic, which would make them easy prey to Islam.[15] The eventual preaching of the gospel is seen as part of the civilizing mission of the French in Africa. Though living as a priest and a holy man among the Tuaregs, he corresponded with General Laperrine about military and cartographical matters: the publication of the letters between the two men, over a period that included the early years of the First World War, provoked some scandalized protests in the 1950s.[16] He was a man of his time, and still something of a former cavalry officer; though not everyone of his time was so naïve – not the Abbé Huvelin who protested against Foucauld's enthusiasm for the car and the railway and how they would transform Africa:

> They talk a lot of the work of unification of the human race by means of communications. Ah! How are things now? They have brought together hatreds and enmities, which have become more venomous, more cruel. Much more quickly one is set against another, one is over against another, one detests another: is that unification?[17]

All that is true, but it is not the deepest truth about Charles de Foucauld. The deeper truth is that all that he had learnt about presence and tenderness and patience informed his life in the desert. The Tuaregs respected him because he respected them and their culture. He would preach Christ not by talking about him, but by his presence, by his prayer. 'I am a *monk* and not a *missionary*, made for silence not for speech . . .'[18] By his silence, and by his presence, he would prepare the tribes of North Africa for the gospel. 'Direct evangelization is impossible at the moment; the only life possible is that of Nazareth, in poverty, abjection, every humiliation, adoration, manual or intellectual work, or a mixture of both, according to what is necessary, what is possible.'[19] By his celebration of the Eucharist, by his prayer, especially before the Sacrament, he would be a witness to the presence of Christ. 'By His presence, Jesus will sanctify, silently, this vast country.'[20] The most effective thing is not to *talk* about realities, but simply to hold oneself in the presence of ultimate Reality, the reality of God the Creator, and to be a vehicle of the utterly real love of God. So as war engulfed Europe,

Charles de Foucauld saw what he was doing, alone in the desert, as not at all irrelevant to the hopes and fears of men and women.

> We live in times when the soul feels strongly the need for prayer. In the storm that blows over Europe, one feels the nothingness of the creature, and one turns towards the Creator . . . Before the Blessed Sacrament, one feels oneself so really in the presence of Being, even though everything created seems, according to all the evidence, to touch nothingness.[21]

This is the spirit of Charles de Foucauld, that has inspired the communities of Little Brothers and Sisters who witness to the presence of Christ where he is forgotten or quite unsuspected – in Africa and India, but also in the cities of secularized western Europe. The way of the desert is not so much flight from society and community, as finding a way to an oasis where one can be aware again of the ultimate reality of God. But it is no easier than the way into the desert, no less demanding, no less costly. If Charles de Foucauld is an example of the way in which the ideal of the desert can still appeal in the twentieth century, it suggests something extreme and uncomfortable. It is no gentle retreat, but a 'movement towards the infinite':[22] an infinite renunciation laying bare the soul before God so that is becomes a 'dry leaf, a grain of dust, a speck of foam'.[23]

This 'movement towards the infinite' that led Charles de Foucauld from the tidy security of life in society – even life in the austere community of la Trappe – to the limitless wastes of the desert could have destroyed him, had he not found a way in which his restless yearning could be certain that it was responding to God and not losing itself in the labyrinth of the human soul. Charles de Foucauld found that way through *obedience*, obedience to the direction of his spiritual father, the Abbé Huvelin. It was, in some ways, a paradoxical obedience. We have seen that his fellow Trappists felt that it was his incapacity for long-term obedience that led to his leaving their order, and as one reads the correspondence between Charles de Foucauld and the Abbé Huvelin, the notion of obedience seems like a game of cat-and-mouse: in the end, what Foucauld does will be done in obedience to Huvelin, but it is rarely what Huvelin himself counselled when asked, rather what he finally acquiesced in as things developed.[24] On one occasion, indeed, when Foucauld eventually left Beni-Abbès, his paradoxical notion of obedience becomes quite explicit: 'I am not leaving so quickly from lack of obedience to you, beloved and venerated Father, but because the most perfect obedience – that which is a part of perfection – means in certain cases that one takes the initiative.'[25] In that case, as in others, Huvelin's counsel 'Remain where you are' becomes acquiescence: 'Follow the movement that compels you, it is not what I would have dreamt of, but I believe that it is what God has said to you.'[26] But such paradoxical obedience was still obedience:[27] it was through opening his heart to Huvelin and listening to his counsel that he tested what God's will was for him, and to that he was finally obedient. But it needed the skilled direction of a Huvelin to guide his 'movement towards the infinite' so that his life in the desert was prevented from becoming a destructive restlessness, and instead became fulfilled in a life of obedience to God.

But who was the Abbé Huvelin? He was in fact a remarkable spiritual director, not just of Charles de Foucauld, but of many others, including Baron von Hügel, whose own writings on prayer and mysticism, and indeed his own work of spiritual direction, have had such a profound influence throughout England, and several distinguished figures in French intellectual life at the turn of the century, among them the great French philosopher Maurice Blondel. As we shall see, desert spirituality and spiritual fatherhood are closely linked, so it is relevant to any attempt to understand the desert spirituality of Charles de Foucauld to consider the spiritual fatherhood of the Abbé Huvelin. But the Abbé Huvelin is even closer to our theme, in that he too can be considered a desert saint, one who dwelt in the desert, only for him it was not a literal desert but the inward wilderness of desolation of his own mind.

He was born at Laon in Picardy on 7 October 1838 and

was baptized eighteen months later at the church of St-Martin in Colmar, in Alsace, by which time his parents had moved to Paris. The delay, and the strange place, of his baptism are probably to be explained by the fact that his father, having been brought up a Catholic, had converted to atheism (his father seems not to have been present at the baptism of his son). Henri, as the future priest was called (his baptismal names were Marie Joseph Philippe), felt called to the priesthood early on, but was opposed in this by his father. The son yielded for a time to his father's wishes, and when he left his lycée, went to the Ecole Normale Supérieure, where he studied history. Shortly before going there Henri Huvelin lost his mother. After leaving the Ecole Normale Supérieure he put off taking up the teaching post expected of a *normalien*, on grounds of ill-health, and went to Rome, where he studied for the priesthood. When he returned to Paris in 1865 he taught for a time at the junior seminary at St-Nicolas du Chardonnet. Ordained priest in 1867, he continued to teach at the junior seminary, and then became a curate at the church of St-Eugène. In 1875 he became curate at the church of St-Augustin, the large, ugly church just north of the Grands Magasins in Paris. There he remained for thirty-five years until his death in 1910. He was very popular as a preacher and a teacher, and much sought-after as a confessor. He hated such celebrity, and must be very satisfied with the neglect that his memory has found in the years since his death (there is no memorial to him at St-Augustin: he is simply mentioned – in small letters – in the memorial to Charles de Foucauld's conversion in the chapel where he used to hear confessions).

Baron von Hügel recalled 'with all the vividness resulting from direct personal intercourse and deep spiritual obligations' the Abbé Huvelin in these words:

A gentleman by birth and breeding, a distinguished Hellenist, a man of exquisitely piercing, humorous mind, he could readily have become a great editor or interpreter of Greek philosophical or patristic texts, or a remarkable Church historian. But this deep and heroic personality deliberately preferred 'to write in souls' whilst occupying, during thirty-five years, a supernumerary, unpaid post in a large Parisian parish. There, suffering from gout in the eyes and brain, and usually lying prone in a darkened room, he served souls with the supreme authority of self-oblivious love, and brought light and purity and peace to countless troubled, sorrowing, or sinful souls.[28]

In the confessional, or in the darkened room of which von Hügel spoke (darkened to make less unbearable the migrainous headaches with which he was usually afflicted – only two good days in three weeks, he mentions once in his diary),[29] Huvelin was visited by many, many people. Most are unknown; but those who are known suggest his remarkable appeal. Apart from Charles de Foucauld and Baron von Hügel, Lucienne Portier, in her remarkable book on Huvelin, discusses his encounters with the famous positivist atheist, Emile Littré, with the ex-priest Hyacinthe Loyson, and with the modernists Loisy, Maurice Blondel and Henri Bremond. What is particularly remarkable is the confidence he could inspire in those who were alienated from the Church, or who found themselves brutally used during the so-called Modernist crisis by the Catholic Church of Pope Pius IX and his successors. What they found in the Abbé Huvelin was not one who took their side against the Church. He was a priest of the Catholic Church, but as a priest he wanted 'to stand in the realm of the charity of Christ, who must give all. If the priest is the man for some people, he diminishes himself, and if he is the man for almost everyone, he is still too small, he must be the man for everyone.'[30] But as a priest he helped those who turned to him to see something of the love of Christ. To Hyacinthe Loyson, the priest who had left the Catholic Church after the proclamation of Papal Infallibility in 1870 and two years later had married, he wrote, 'I did not want to convert you, but to show you that in the Church of God there are souls who love, who will go to any length in searching, who seek what our Lord sought.'[31]

But this great work of spiritual direction, a work he often found unbearably burdensome, was carried out by one who felt on his own shoulders, in his own heart, an almost unbearable burden of suffering of his own. His letters and diary reveal one who knew endless misery, and often found his thoughts turning towards death – as release, and suicide as the means. The enormous demands of preaching, teaching, caring for the sick and dying, hour after hour in the confessional, added to the continual burden of suffering, physical and mental, the encroachment of despair and depression: all this produced an intense weariness. Weariness, nothing more, he said to himself, not the suffering of reparation, of sharing Christ's suffering: a weariness that seemed to undermine his reason and threaten to topple him over into madness. 'I am not any better than last week, I have studied my case in other people, I assure you, there is nothing supernatural about it, just excessive fatigue, and just as in madness each one manifests habitual preoccupations, boundless sadness and the thought of suicide.'[32]

To others, Huvelin could speak of the value of suffering. He spoke to von Hügel of 'souls who can understand, quite individual souls, who have suffered a great deal':[33] suffering deepens the soul, makes it capable of understanding, sympathy, compassion. In this way he explained the suffering of Christ and his cross:

Jesus wanted to suffer because suffering is the great problem, the great objection. There is nothing more terrible than that which comes out of an unhappy heart . . . Why does He suffer? Why is He on the cross? It is for you, to be with you, so that you cannot complain of suffering . . . Yes, the great cry that rose from the cross to penetrate Heaven, like the cry of suffering of the whole of humanity, that cry was uttered so that you could mix yours with it, so that your suffering, purified in its source, purified in the suffering of that One, might become as triumphant and powerful as Him. That is the 'why' of the cross. Now dare to complain . . . Christ, in making the heart greater and more capable of great things, has at the same time made it more capable of feeling suffering . . . He has made the heart capable of suffering. He has transformed suffering.

To suffer with Christ is to be more extended in charity, it is to feel more the sufferings of others and to press them to the heart. The more one suffers, the more one understands that souls are, more than anything else, beings that suffer and that need to be consoled and relieved, rather than punished and corrected.

Suffering makes us greater than we would ever wish to be ourselves.[34]

It was this sense of suffering that gave to Huvelin's dealings with souls his gentleness and understanding. And this sense of suffering was learnt by his own suffering. But whereas, faced with the suffering of others, he sought to console and relieve, his own suffering seemed rather to drive him to the brink of madness and despair.

One of the most curious things amongst Huvelin's papers are whole pages (or the top of a page, or its borders) filled with what look like doodles: his name 'Huvelin' written out time and again, sometimes with a capital H, sometimes with a small h, sometimes in a calligraphic hand, sometimes printed, sometimes scribbled, often decorated with flourishes and patterns. In one case, a section of 'Huvelins' at the top of a page is covered with a grill of fine ruled lines, horizontal, vertical and diagonal: a grill that imprisons the repeated name? Sometimes something else is written: '*Huv il était*', and a little lower down '*J'étais Huvelin*' with a long backward flourish which swerves back and encloses '*tu étais, il était*' and another 'Huvelin' decorated with elaborate flourishes. In another place, at the bottom of a column of 'Huvelins', in tiny writing, scarcely legible, there is written '*il n'est*'. What does all this mean? A kind of perpetual self-verification? A dizzying search for his own identity, the identity of one tormentedly drawn to self-doubt and self-destruction? Should we recall St Catherine of Siena's 'I am He who is, you are she who is not', that Huvelin was familiar with and often quoted in his lectures? Even if we do recall Catherine's saying, we should not, I think, let it tempt us into reading these scribbles as expressing a 'pious' sense of non-existence in relation to God: the obsessive, anguished character of these doodles seems to point to a genuine sense of inner desolation, verging on madness and a depressive longing for annihilation. It seems to suggest that Huvelin lived in an inner wildnerness, a desert within, that

– like the literal desert – afforded him no sense of security, no place of comfort. It suggests we should see Huvelin as a desert saint struggling in a barren place, inhabited by demons quite as terrifying as any St Antony faced. That his inner struggle was fruitful is manifest in the value so many people found in his priestly ministry: and perhaps that ministry bore such great fruit precisely *because* the inner struggle in the desert of his mind was so unrelenting.[35]

We can perhaps suggest some ways in which the desert spirituality of the Abbé Huvelin found expression in his spiritual direction. The barrenness of the desert conveys a strong sense of the futility of human effort: nothing much can be achieved there by human means. It speaks of despair, but beyond despair it can speak of what can only be achieved by God: when the prophet wants to speak of God's redeeming activity, he says that 'the desert shall rejoice, and blossom as the rose' (Isa. 35:1). For Huvelin spiritual direction has nothing to do with trying to advise people, trying to shape their lives: rather the spiritual father tries to help those who turn to him to respond to God, to let God work within them. So in criticism of Jansenism, he said:

> There exist families of souls which are determined to find the principle of tranquillity within their own selves; they want to cast anchor within their own depths. But we have to cast anchor, not below, but above; it is in God, in His goodness, that we have to found our hope.[36]

Or apropos the spiritual direction of the Abbé Olier, the founder of the seminary of St-Sulpice: 'The world sees, in this or that soul, the passions, the bitter waters that fill it; but we priests, we seek the little spring of sweet waters, Arethusa, that little thread of grace, which, though deeper down and more hidden, is nevertheless most truly there.'[37] Charles de Foucauld found that the desert was no place for success: he achieved little, apart from being there; he converted no one. But he had learnt from Abbé Huvelin not to seek success: echoing the abbé's words to him, he said of his vocation in the desert, 'It is not at all a matter of making a success.'[38] Quesnel, speaking of Huvelin's direction in relation to Charles de Foucauld, quotes some of his remarks about conversion in his discussion of the Abbé de Rancé, the founder of the Trappists: 'No, suffering alone does not lead to conversion. There is needed the work of grace . . . There is in a conversion, something divine, impossible to explain.'[39] Quesnel goes on to say,

> All is grace in a conversion, since it is the irruption of love in a liberty that embraces and releases. The confessor prepares the way back to the mercy of God, he facilitates the encounter with God, and inclines the soul to obey Him, but he cannot ask or demand obedience to his directives. He is a precursor (*précurseur*) and not the Master.[40]

He is a precursor: one who goes before, a forerunner of Christ, like John the Baptist, who also lived in the desert. The same point is made by Lucienne Portier in the title of her book: *Un Précurseur, l'abbé Huvelin*. The forerunner, the voice in the wilderness: such desert imagery points to the nature of spiritual fatherhood, at least as Huvelin understood it.[41]

In other ways the barrenness of the desert points to the nature of spiritual direction. Its very barrenness suggests that growth is difficult and delicate, ultimately only possible with the irrigation of divine grace, but even then still a delicate matter. There are lots of hints of such delicacy in the Abbé Huvelin's teaching. 'The will to love, regret at not loving: that is already something of love.'[42] Or, as he said apropos St Francis de Sales: 'a spirituality of little-by-little is not an enfeebled spirituality'.[43] On the other hand the desert is a place of solitude: in the desert there is not the support that can be provided by society, by being with other people, not even the support of other Christians. This freedom from support was something Huvelin valued for itself: so he advised the young Baron von Hügel, 'No Catholic reunions, no societies: if the building can go up without scaffolding, so much the better.'[44]

There is a great difference between the types of desert spirituality we have just begun to explore – those of Charles de Foucauld and the Abbé Huvelin – though there is a strong link between them in the bond of spiritual fatherhood that bound Huvelin to Foucauld. The desert *attracted* Charles de Foucauld, from the time before his conversion when it was a challenge that drew out his soul and gave it a taste for the 'movement towards the infinite', throughout his life as a Christian, where the desert became more and more a symbol of the poverty that the Son of God embraced in the incarnation, the poverty that is the lot of those who know nothing of the love of God, and the vocation of those determined to know nothing but the love of God. The way of the desert became his way of 'following nakedly the naked Christ' (to use Jerome's expression). The desert was, for Charles de Foucauld, a place of spiritual experience, not in the sense of making for spiritual 'highs', but rather in the sense of requiring a stripping down of his life so that all that was left was awareness of the reality of God, and adoration. Huvelin's desert was rather different: the barrenness of the mental desert he inhabited was not something he *chose*, but something he endured. But in both cases the desert became a fruitful place: in both cases the grace of God made 'the desert rejoice and blossom as a rose'. In Charles de Foucauld's case by the appeal of his life and his spirituality; in Huvelin's case, by the great blessing other people reaped from his closeness to God and his sensitivity to the souls that turned to him. The appeal of Charles de Foucauld lies, one may guess, in the uncompromising yearning for the infinite, in the generosity of his self-giving, in the sense that extreme situations call for extreme remedies, in the gentleness and simplicity that breathes through his spiritual writings. The blessings of the Abbé Huvelin's direction are the sort that are easily lost sight of, as is the case with other spiritual directors, for example, more recently, the Anglican priest Reginald Somerset Ward.[45] Their writings (in Huvelin's case, all posthumous, compiled from the notes of those who heard him; in Somerset Ward's case, all published anonymously) do not convey – we can well believe – the extraordinary impression their words of personal counsel left with those who turned to them. In both cases they chose to 'write in souls' (as Huvelin said of Père de Condren), souls that are difficult for others to read, and have now mostly passed to eternity. It reminds us that much that is most important in reality is quite particular, and escapes the generalizing glance of those who rely on books. It is tantalizing, but also perhaps humbling.

NOTES

Charles de Foucauld was first made known to the wider world by René Bazin's excellent biography (*Charles de Foucauld, explorateur au Maroc, ermite au Sahara*, Paris, 1921; Eng. tr., 1923), which quotes extensively from his papers and correspondence. Bazin also published a small selection of Foucauld's spiritual writings, *Ecrits spirituels de Charles de Foucauld* (1923; Eng. tr., 1930). There is a much larger anthology ed. Denise Barrat, *Oeuvres spirituelles de Charles de Jésus* (Paris, 1958). All his papers – mainly meditations which he wrote out – are in the process of being published, ed. B. Jacqueline, the postulator in the cause of his canonization (Paris, 1973 ff). A valuable account of his life through his letters and papers has been compiled by J.-F. Six (*Itinéraire spirituel de Charles de Foucauld*, Paris, 1958; Eng. tr., 1964), who has also edited his correspondence with the Abbé Huvelin (*Correspondance Père de Foucauld–Abbé Huvelin*, Tournai, 1957). There is a fine study of Foucauld by Roger Quesnel, *Charles de Foucauld: les etapes d'une recherche* (Tours, 1966).

Nothing of Huvelin's was published during his lifetime (apart from an article on Theodoret the Church historian): what has been published since his death has been variously unsatisfactory (see Portier, cited below, pp. 259–68). Marie-Thérèse (Louis-)Lefebvre, who has published two collections of Huvelin's writings (*Ecrits spirituels*, 1959, and a collection of sermons, *Venez et Voyez*, 1961), has also published a life (*Un prêtre, l'abbé Huvelin*, enlarged edn, 1958; Eng. tr., 1967). Huvelin was memorialized in a few pages at the end of Baron von Hügel's *Eternal Life* (Edinburgh, 1912), pp. 374–7; and his remarks to the young von Hügel over a few days in May 1886, when the baron sought his spiritual advice, were printed in *Selected Letters 1896–1924*, ed. B. Holland (London, 1927), pp. 58–63. I have made use of Huvelin's volume of lectures, *Quelques directeurs d'âmes au XVIIe siècle* (Paris, edn 4, 1923), but in the main I have relied on Lucienne Portier's splendid biographical study, *Un précurseur: l'abbé Huvelin* (Paris, 1979).

1 Letter to Huvelin (5.xi.90): *Correspondance*, p. 5.
2 *Reconnaissance au Maroc* (Paris, 1888).
3 For the account of Foucauld's conversion, see Bazin, pp. 93 f.

4 Letter from Dom Louis de Gonzague, Foucauld's prior in his last months as a Trappist, quoted in Quesnel, p. 215.
5 See Bazin, pp. 136–45; Quesnel, pp. 43–66.
6 Bazin, pp. 151 f.
7 ibid. p. 152.
8 Quoted in ibid. p. 97.
9 Letters to Foucauld (9.xii.97): *Correspondance*, p. 56 (quoted in Quesnel, p. 75).
10 Letter to Foucauld (18.ii.98): *Correspondance*, pp. 69 f (quoted in Quesnel, p. 74).
11 For the importance of the mystery of the Visitation for Foucauld, see Quesnel, pp. 76–80.
12 See ibid. p. 101, and *Oeuvres spirituelles*, pp. 531 f (which he cites).
13 On the Little Brothers and Sisters, see R. Voillaume, *Au Coeur des Masses: La vie religieuse des petits frères du Père de Foucauld* (Paris, 1952); abridged Eng. tr. as *Seeds of the Desert* (1955).
14 Bazin, p. 353.
15 ibid. pp. 346–51.
16 See the remarks of Père Rétif in his review of the correspondence between Foucauld and Laperrine (*Lettres au Général Laperrine*, Paris, 1955) in *Etudes*, 286 (1956), quoted in Quesnel, p. 168n.
17 Quoted in Portier, pp. 103 f.
18 Quoted by Bazin, p. 348.
19 Letter (1.x.06) to Mgr Caron (quoted in Quesnel, p. 126).
20 Quoted in Quesnel, p. 123.
21 Quoted in Bazin, p. 450.
22 Letter to Foucauld (2.viii.96); *Correspondance*, p. 41.
23 *Oeuvres spirituelles*, p. 761 (quoted in Quesnel, p. 188).
24 See the *Correspondance Foucauld–Huvelin* and Six's *Itinéraire spirituel*; also Portier's discussion, pp. 93–107.
25 Letter to Huvelin (26.viii.03), quoted in Portier, p. 106.
26 Huvelin's reply, quoted in ibid.
27 See Quesnel, part 2, esp. pp. 201–60.
28 F. von Hügel, *Eternal Life* (Edinburgh, 1912), pp. 374 f.
29 Portier, p. 35.
30 ibid. p. 150.
31 ibid. p. 64.
32 ibid. p. 43.
33 From the first of the sayings of Abbé Huvelin from the advice he gave to Baron von Hügel: *Selected Letters*, p. 58.
34 Portier, p. 212.

35 See ibid. pp. 41–8, and the pages of scribbles reproduced in her book, facing p. 164, and between pp. 269 and 270.
36 *Quelques directeurs d'âmes*, pp. 36 f (quoted in von Hügel, *Eternal Life*, p. 375).
37 ibid. p. 111 (quoted in von Hügel, p. 376).
38 Quoted in Quesnel, p. 103, who points out that Foucauld's words here echo those of Huvelin to him (ibid. n.80).
39 *Quelques directeurs*, p. 228 (quoted in von Hügel, p. 377).
40 Quesnel, pp. 16 f.
41 See Huvelin's sermon-notes on John the Baptist, discussed and quoted in Portier, pp. 161–4.
42 Portier, p. 235.
43 *Quelques directeurs*, p. 12 (quoted in von Hügel, p. 375).
44 *Selected Letters*, p. 60.
45 See E. R. Morgan, *Reginald Somerset Ward 1881–1962* (London, 1963).

2

The Desert in the Bible

'All the great religions were born between the desert and the steppe,' says Carlo Carretto, somewhere.[1] One thinks of Muhammad's retreats to Mount Hira' in the Arabian desert, and the revelation to him there of what eventually became the Qur'an; or of the Buddha's departure from his father's palace to the forests and waste lands of Northern India. The Bible too supports such an idea of the desert as the place where God reveals himself to men and women: think of Moses on Mount Sinai in the wilderness of Sin (Exod. 19 ff), or of Elijah's encounter with God on the same mountain (on this occasion called Horeb: 1 Kings 19:8); or of John the Baptist, the Forerunner, 'preaching in the wilderness of Judea' (Matt: 3:1), or of the place of desert solitude in the life of Jesus himself, where he was tempted for forty days before the beginning of his ministry (Matt. 4:1–11 and parallels), where he often retreated to pray to his Father (Luke 4:42, 6:12, 9:18, 11:1, etc.), and where on Mount Tabor (or perhaps Mount Hermon)[2] he was transfigured (Mark 9:2–8 and parallels).

It is worth, then, spending some time looking at the desert, and what it means in the story of God's dealings with men and women in the Bible. Perhaps the first thing to notice is that the desert is not an ultimate symbol: the desert is encountered in the course of the story many times, but the story neither begins there, nor does it end there. The story the Bible tells begins with a garden, the garden of Eden, paradise (which is the Greek for a garden): a garden is pleasant, filled with flowers and fruits and streams and fountains, not at all barren or harsh. At least this garden was:

26

And the Lord God planted a garden in Eden, in the east; and there he put the man whom he had formed. And out of the ground the Lord God made to grow every tree that is pleasant to the sight and good for food, the tree of life also in the midst of the garden, and the tree of the knowledge of good and evil. A river flowed out of Eden to water the garden . . . (Gen. 2:8–10)

It was in such a pleasant place that men and women were to live together, according to the story at the beginning of the Bible. They were to enjoy themselves and be happy there. Nor does the Bible end with a desert: the apostle John sees a *city*:

And I saw the holy city, new Jerusalem, coming down out of heaven from God, prepared as a bride adorned for her husband; and I heard a loud voice from the throne saying, 'Behold, the dwelling of God is with men. He will dwell with them, and they shall be his people, and God himself will be with them, he will wipe away every tear from their eyes, and death shall be no more . . . (Rev. 21:2–4)

The final goal to which the apostle, the prophet, looks is a city, at harmony with God, its citizens at harmony with one another, a place where there is no misery, no death. Mention of the city as a bride reminds one of that strange little book in the Old Testament, the Song of Songs, a celebration of the love of a bride and a bridegroom, a celebration of love devoid of shame or fear, the love that Adam and Eve were meant to share in their garden, as the Song of Songs itself is set in a garden (see 4:12, 5:1, etc.).

It is between the garden and the city that we find the desert. Adam and Eve are driven out of the garden, as a result of their sin, essentially the sin of disobedience: the garden is no longer something given to them as a place to enjoy and live in. The land was to be worked: it has to be tilled and planted, now with much effort it brings forth food and 'in the sweat of your face, you shall eat bread'. If man fails to till the ground and care for it, it becomes barren, hostile – a desert. The desert is a threat, a warning, a spur to activity, between the garden of Eden and the city of God. The early chapters of Genesis sketch – no more than that – man's attempts to keep the desert at bay: the descendants of Adam live as nomads, in tents (see Gen. 4:20); they learn how to make tools and weapons from bronze and iron (cf. 4:22), to cheer up their threatened existence with music (cf. 4:21). The cursed nature of human life driven from the garden manifests itself in Cain's murder of Abel, and more decisively in a settled wickedness that is swept away by the flood. A new start is made with Noah. This time, the fable suggests, humankind bids for more than a nomadic existence, this time they band together and start to build a city: not the city of God the apostle will see, 'coming down out of heaven from God', but a city rising from the earth, having 'a tower with its top in the heavens' (Gen. 11:4), a monument of human defiance of God. This city, this tower, of Babel is thwarted by the 'confusion of tongues', the creation of mutual incomprehension by the diversity of human languages.

Humankind, banished from the garden, tries to protect itself against the encroachment of the desert by resort to a city, an earthly city, founded by humans banding together to create a sense of self-sufficiency. In the biblical story there is set against that those who dare to go out into the desert, who dare to rely on God alone, who dare to abandon the illusion of human self-sufficiency and live in obedience to God.

The first . . . the first was really Noah. The sea – the flood – perhaps even more than the desert, speaks of a region of life beyond human capacity to control. The ark, borne up by the waters that engulf human civilization – an ark built in obedience to God's command, so big that it seemed humanly useless: what more powerful symbol could one have for the abandonment of human self-sufficiency and reliance on God alone?

But Noah is an isolated example, almost a false start. The series of venturers really begins with Abraham. 'Now the Lord said to Abram, "Go from your country and your kindred and your father's house to the land that I will show you" . . . So Abram went . . . and journeyed on, still going towards the Negeb' (Gen. 12:1, 4, 9): the Negeb, or the Negev, the great desert to the south of the Holy Land. Abraham's life is

28

presented as a life of obedience, not obedience to some humanly understandable calculation, but obedience to the Unknown, the unknowable God, obedience in faith, 'the conviction of things not seen' (Heb. 11:1). So the author of the letter to the Hebrews says:

> By faith Abraham obeyed when he was called to go out to a place which he was to receive as an inheritance; and he went out, not knowing where he was to go. By faith he sojourned in the land of promise, as in a foreign land, living in tents with Isaac and Jacob, heirs with him of the same promise. For he looked forward to the city which has foundations, whose builder and maker is God. By faith Sarah herself received power to conceive, even when she was past the age, since she considered him faithful who had promised. Therefore from one man, and him as good as dead, were born descendants as many as the stars of heaven and as the innumerable grains of sand by the seashore. (Heb. 11:8–12)

In faith in the unknown God and in obedience to him, Abraham leaves his house and goes out into a foreign land, travelling through the desert, in search of the city, 'whose builder and maker is God'.

That is the first lesson the desert teaches: relinquishment of human society and human control and dependence on God alone. It is not anti-human as such; it is a matter of priorities. What will come of all this is the reconstitution of a human society, the 'city which has foundations': but that will only be realized if God is the first priority. And that will only be achieved by the relinquishing of human attempts to fend for ourselves, to control and fashion our environment and our society.

But it is in the story of Moses and the account of the Exodus that the desert becomes a central theme. Moses' survival as a baby was the result of his parents' relinquishing any human attempt to save him, and trusting to providence, to God. The baby in the basket made of bulrushes is discovered by Pharaoh's daughter, who brings him up as her son. But the beginning of Moses' own encounter with God takes place in the wilderness, where Moses is looking after his father-in-law's flock of sheep after he has fled from Egypt. He comes to Horeb (which scholars identify with Mount Sinai, at the south of the Sinai Peninsula):

> And the angel of the Lord appeared to him in a flame of fire out of the midst of a bush; and he looked, and lo, the bush was burning, yet it was not consumed. And Moses said, 'I will turn aside and see this great sight, why the bush is not burnt.' When the Lord saw that he turned aside to see, God called to him out of the bush, 'Moses, Moses!' And he said, 'Here am I.' Then he said, 'Do not come near; put off your shoes from your feet, for the place on which you are standing is holy ground.' And he said, 'I am the God of your father, the God of Abraham, the God of Isaac, and the God of Jacob.' And Moses hid his face, for he was afraid to look at God. (Exod. 3:2–6)

It is in the desert, alone, that Moses encounters – or rather is encountered by – God. At the miracle of the burning bush Moses knows an overwhelming sense of the holiness of the place, such that he feels impelled to remove his shoes. And then God commands Moses to be the instrument by which he will save the people of Israel from the Egyptian oppression. Moses hesitates, asks for God's credentials, and hears God's mysterious revelation as 'I am who I am': beyond definition by any comparison or contrast, but One who simply is . . . who he is – not one understood in terms of other things, but the One in terms of whom everything else finds its meaning. The desert seems a fitting place for such a revelation: the desert, itself devoid of anything in terms of which any comparison might be made, the desert whose barrenness matches, by contrast, the transcendent fulness of God.

Moses comes back from his solitary encounter with God at Mount Horeb to Egypt, to persuade Pharaoh to set free the people of Israel. The request, however, has a specific form, which again involves the desert. Moses asks, 'Thus says the Lord, the God of Israel, "Let my people go, that they may hold a feast to me in the wilderness."' (Exod. 5:1) God's people are to be released so that they may go into the desert and worship their God. The desert symbolizes the relinquishing of human concerns so that God alone can be their sole concern: and such an act of acknowledgement of God as our sole concern, not just our greatest concern, that in terms of which all other concerns are to be understood and become concerns at all – such an act of acknowledgement of God is worship, the worship of One who says 'I am who I am'. The desert enables us to glimpse something of the transcendence of God, something too easily lost sight of amid the concerns of human society.

The Exodus, the crossing of the Red Sea, led the people of Israel into the wilderness, the desert. The Pentateuch tells of forty years in the desert, forty years in which the people of Israel were directly, miraculously, dependent on God for the sustenance. We read of the provision of manna and quails; we read how those who attempted to temper reliance on divine providence with human prudence by gathering more than was necessary for one day were thwarted: for what they had left over the next day had become rotten (Exod. 16:16–21). 'Give us this day our daily bread'; 'Therefore do not be anxious about tomorrow, for tomorrow will be anxious for itself. Let the day's own trouble be sufficient for the day' (Matt. 6:11, 34). Again the relinquishment of anxious human calculation for trust in God.

The desert was for Moses, and through him for the whole of Israel, the place where they lived in dependence on God and where God revealed himself. On Mount Sinai (as it is now called), God reveals himself to Moses in a theophany more dramatic even than the burning bush:

And Mount Sinai was wrapped in smoke, because the Lord descended upon it in fire; and the smoke of it went up like the smoke of a kiln, and the whole mountain quaked greatly. And as the sound of the trumpet grew louder and louder, Moses spoke, and God answered him in thunder. (Exod. 19:18–19)

There follows the revelation of the Law, the Torah, beginning with the Ten Commandments. On another occasion, Moses and the seventy elders go up together on to the mountain:

31

and they saw the God of Israel; and there was under his feet as it were a pavement of sapphire stone, like the very heaven for clearness. And he did not lay his hand on the chief men of the people of Israel; they beheld God, and ate and drank. (Exod. 24:10–11)

This occasion, the celebration of the covenant made between God and Israel in which God reveals his will to Israel so that they can live in peace and harmony with him, is regarded by the biblical writer as something remarkable: God, whose presence is so intense as to overwhelm puny human beings (cf. Gen. 32:30, Judg. 6:22 f, etc.), has allowed human beings to eat and drink in his presence.

Moses is told how to celebrate that 'presence': long chapters describe the decorations for the tent of the Lord's presence (Exod. 25–27), and further chapters set out the sacrificial ceremonies (Exod. 28–30). In that tent, pitched outside the camp, away from the human concerns of society, even a society so closely dependent on God, God revealed his presence and spoke with Moses:

When Moses entered the tent, the pillar of cloud would descend and stand at the door of the tent, and the Lord would speak with Moses. And when all the people saw the pillar of cloud standing at the door of the tent, all the people would rise up and worship, every man at his tent door. Thus the Lord used to speak to Moses face to face, as a man speaks to his friend. (Exod. 33:9–11)

But though, in this period in the desert, God *speaks* to Moses 'face to face' as a friend, Moses is not permitted to 'see' God's face. Later on in the same chapter Moses asks to see God's 'glory', but is told, 'you cannot see my face; for man shall not see me and live' (33:20). Instead God places Moses in the cleft of a rock and 'while my glory passes by . . . I will cover you with my hand until I have passed by; then I will take away my hand, and you shall see my back; but my face shall not be seen' (33:22).

Later generations, Jesus' near-contemporary Philo, the Alexandrian Jew, and following him many of the Christian

Fathers, saw Moses' encounter with God in the wilderness as
a kind of archetype of any human encounter between God
and human beings. Several, especially St Gregory, Bishop of
Nyssa in the latter part of the fourth century, were struck by
how Moses' encounter with God is at once an encounter of
great intimacy and yet an encounter that becomes ever more
mysterious. The light of the burning bush yields to the clouds
and darkness of Sinai and the culmination seems to be God's
turning his back on Moses altogether. Gregory himself interpreted this in terms of God's ultimate unknowability: the
closer we come, the less we seem to know, the more baffling
and surprising God becomes.[3] Others interpreted God's 'back'
as his creative works – not himself, but what he does – or
those works in which God's revelation seems to take the
form of concealment, especially the events of Christ's passion
(Exod. 33:11–23 is one of the readings at vespers on Good
Friday in the Byzantine Rite.)

The story of the forty years in the desert is not just a story
of closeness to God and God's self-revealing: it tells also of
frequent grumbling on the part of the Israelites, and of
attempts to forsake God, culminating in the story of the
golden calf (Exod. 32). None the less the period of the wandering in the wilderness, in contrast to the period that followed
when, according to the biblical account, the Israelites began
to settle in Palestine, is often regarded by the later prophetic
tradition as a kind of golden age. Renewal of the covenant,
so often breached by Israel, is frequently seen in terms of a
return to the desert. This can be alluded to by the form of
the narrative, as in the story of Elijah, who, in fear of Jezebel
after his dramatic victory over the priests of Baal at Mount
Carmel, fled into the desert to Mount Horeb. There, at the
place where the covenant had originally been established,
God reveals himself once again to his prophet:

And he said, 'Go forth, and stand upon the mount before
the Lord.' And behold, the Lord passed by, and a great
and strong wind rent the mountains, and broke into pieces
the rocks before the Lord, but the Lord was not in the
wind; and after the wind an earthquake, but the Lord was
not in the earthquake; and after the earthquake a fire, but

33

the Lord was not in the fire; and after the fire a still small voice. And when Elijah heard it, he wrapped his face in his mantle and went out and stood at the entrance to the cave. (1 Kgs 19:11–13)

It is very different from the dramatic revelation of God to Moses on Mount Sinai. Here the dramatic manifestations of God's power are not manifestations of his presence; his presence is manifested in a 'still small voice' (or, according to the Greek Septuagint and the Latin Vulgate, the 'sound of a gentle breeze'), something that could easily be missed except in the silence of the desert. It is a moment of reassurance for Elijah, a turning-point. He returns from Horeb, finds a disciple in Elisha, and there begin to unfold the events that will lead to the overthrow of King Ahab, faithless to the God of Israel under the influence of his wife Jezebel.

Or the idea of a return to the desert can be quite explicit. Hosea's prophecy presents God as saying to Israel:

Therefore, behold, I will allure her, and bring her into the wilderness, and speak tenderly to her. And there I will give her her vineyards, and make the Valley of Achor a door of hope. And there she shall answer as in the days of her youth, as at the time when she came out of the land of Egypt. (Hos. 2:14–16)

God's covenant with Israel, seen as a love-pact, will be renewed where it was first made: in the desert. The wilderness is seen as a kind of trysting-place, a secret place lovers can resort to – a secret place, away from any distractions, where God can woo his beloved, Israel.

A barren place, a secret place, a place that humans can make nothing of themselves, where only God can do anything. It is in these terms that Moses sings of God's dealings with his people (seen as masculine this time) in his song:

He found him in a desert land, and in the howling waste of the wilderness; he encircled him, he cared for him, he kept him as the apple of his eye. Like an eagle that stirs up its nest, that flutters over its young, spreading out its wings, catching them, bearing them on its pinions, the Lord alone did lead him . . . (Deut. 32:10–12)

But the place in the prophetic writings where the imagery of the desert is most developed is in those parts of Isaiah that belong to a later prophet of the Exilic period:

> The wilderness and the dry land shall be glad,
>   the desert shall rejoice and blossom;
> like the crocus it shall blossom abundantly,
>   and rejoice with joy and singing.
> The glory of Lebanon shall be given to it,
>   the majesty of Carmel and Sharon.
> They shall see the glory of the Lord,
>   the majesty of our God . . .
> For waters shall break forth in the wilderness,
>   and steams in the desert;
> the burning sand shall become a pool,
>   and the thirsty ground springs of water . . .
>
> Isa. 35:1–3, 6–7

> Hearken to me, you who pursue deliverance,
>   you who seek the Lord;
> look to the rock from which you were hewn,
>   and to the quarry from which you were digged . . .
> For the Lord will comfort Zion;
>   he will comfort all her waste places,
> and will make her wilderness like Eden,
>   her desert like the garden of the Lord;
> joy and gladness will be found in her,
>   thanksgiving and the voice of song.
>
> Isa. 51:1, 3; cf. 41:17–20

Here it is not just the desert's being a place where God's presence is manifest, rather that God's power is manifest in the transformation of the desert: the barren desert is transformed by God into Eden, the garden of paradise. The desert becomes a kind of natural analogy to the human poor, who are seen in the Bible as those dependent on God, and thus those able to receive his grace and be rewarded with it.

'Blessed are the poor, for theirs is the kingdom of God': blessed is the desert, for it shall become paradise.

The desert, barren for human purposes, is open to divine purposes. So, as the time of the New Covenant begins to dawn, its herald, John the Baptist, appears in the desert. But John the Baptist is more than a prophet *from* the desert, he is a prophet *of* the desert. This is something the Abbé Huvelin brought out in his sermons on St John the Baptist:

> Him whom no-one knows – 30 years of Nazareth – of this obliteration – a *deep horror of being something* – Ecce agnus Dei! Who are you, then?
>
> A voice – nothing much – a glass from which the liquid has been drunk – and good to break . . . the thought when it has been uttered . . . a nothing that disappears, that vanishes.
>
> There goes out quite strongly this voice from the bosom of this penitence, this austerity – this life which means nothing to the world . . . His whole being is a voice – it must be great so that such a voice should emerge from it. Which speaks of God.
>
> How rightly he calls himself a voice. He is there to *shout it*, in fact. They take him for Him! He suddenly shakes to the root of his being like one demented – hypocrite, lie, to carry the weight of esteem – John the Baptist is quick to clear himself – he needs to confess it. I will undeceive you. If that then everything would be lost! What is a voice? A voice that breaks out. Humble – a cry that *dies as it is uttered*. What it bears remains – but it dies – But greatness . . .
>
> *A voice*. It is nothing. It is a great deal – It breaks out – but it has said a word – the power of a voice.
>
> A voice, oh it's nothing much. It breaks out, is dissipated, disappears. Yes – but if it leaves one in front of the truth that was before and will be afterwards. Eternal victory.[4]

John the Baptist *incorporates* the desert, its nothingness, its barrenness, in being a voice: a sound, bearing a meaning, nothing in itself. And in being that, John becomes a model for every Christian. Because John incorporates the desert, not just in lifestyle, but in his very being, he becomes the vehicle for God's purposes, the messenger, the forerunner, the one who points to Christ. One thinks of the long, bony finger of Matthias Grünewald's John the Baptist in the Isenheim altarpiece, or of the figure of the Baptist at the side of the icon-screen, drawing one's eyes over to the right, to the figure of Christ on the right of the holy doors.

And the desert, we have seen, has a place in the life of our Lord himself. After his baptism he is driven out into the wilderness by the Spirit (Mark 1:12): 'And he was in the wilderness forty days, tempted by Satan; and he was with the wild beasts; and the angels ministered to him' (Mark 1:13). Mark's account of our Lord's temptation is much less detailed than that to be found in Matthew and Luke. But it brings out more sharply, perhaps, the place of the desert: a place away from the city, away from human concerns, even good and worthwhile human concerns, a place inhabited by non-humans – by wild beasts, by the angels, by Satan. It makes more sense, perhaps, to us to interpret this as Jesus' being alone with himself, with his human fears and hopes. Many people cannot bear being alone for very long, and so they take care that they are never really alone. Even if they have no one with them, they blunt the edge of the solitude with the radio or television, personal stereo or whatever – with distraction, with something to divert and entertain. Something to cheer us up – or rather, something to blunt our deep longing for real happiness, a happiness that would come from within, rather than being snatched – and let slip – from outside. 'I have often said,' Pascal tells us, 'that the sole cause of man's unhappiness is that he does not know how to stay quietly in his room.'[5]

Jesus' life, as presented to us in the gospels, especially St Luke's, is punctuated by periods of solitude: the forty days at the beginning of his ministry, periods of early morning prayer before the disciples have woken up, his time of solitary prayer in the Garden of Gethsemane before his arrest. And they are *long* periods of solitary prayer – days and hours, not minutes. It is not surprising that those who have been drawn to follow Christ closely have similarly been drawn to such periods of solitary prayer, and to the desert that furnishes conditions for such prayer, nor that the Church has found that some of its members, for the sake of the whole Body, have found their vocation in the desert.

If we look at the desert in Jesus' life, as portrayed in the gospels, several things are striking. First, Jesus returns again and again to the desert, although his ministry was a ministry to men and women, where they are, in villages and in the city. One such occasion was the transfiguration, when Jesus withdrew with the inner group of the disciples, Peter, James and John, and went up a 'high mountain apart by themselves; and he was transfigured before them' (Mark 9:2). Among the papers of the Abbé Huvelin, there are several meditations of the Transfiguration, doubtless material for sermons. One draws together the desert in which Jesus was tempted, and the desert where Mount Tabor stood:

Why not?
The desert – with wild beasts –
    I understand

(a) The Temptation. I feel myself deeply engaged in that combat.

(b) But what has this brilliance to do with me, this brilliant whiteness

Objection   On this poor earth, between the dust that soils our feet – and the clouds where one loses one's head, where the sight troubles and confounds!

(c) To speak of the transfiguration in the midst of this life which disfigures

Response   Undeceive yourself! You are also deeply engaged in this glory

(a) The Son of man so that we might become sons of God.
                                                This is the Son!
     Don't speak evil of life. It has had its sorrow. The Universe

(b) In order to have a happy world. But great

But that of which we complain is not that which God
has made – but that which we have made in defiance
of God – the consequences of our faults –

(c) Despair – the most dangerous temptation destroyed
by his criticisms at all points of contact.

And the meditation continues, concluding:

> He who loves – changes also
> Look closer. Jesus. Life –

Let us take hold. Let us do the work of transformation.
Come and you will see. And we shall enter into the meaning
of the mystery. We shall not see anything of it – but the
others – perhaps not even the believers – but those who
feel some kinship – and things will appear to us to be
almost true – and we shall recognize![6]

The freedom the desert gives, that we know when we are
confronted with ourselves and do not despair: that freedom
opens our eyes to see the glory of Christ revealed on the
mount, revealed as the Son, our brother.

Another thing we notice as we look at the desert in Jesus'
life is that the desert is not always a *literal* desert. We have
mentioned Gethsemane as a place where Jesus prayed alone.
That was no desert: it was a garden. But it was night, and
Jesus was alone (the disciples were asleep): the experience in
the garden recapitulates the experience of the temptations in
the desert, refining Christ's human will to closer and closer
obedience to his divine will, the will of his Father. On a
human level, it would seem that the sought solitude of Jesus'
life prepared him for this moment when he accepted the
chalice with the whole of his being: 'Father, if thou art willing,
remove this cup from me; nevertheless not my will, but thine,
be done.' The night of Gethsemane was the last desert Jesus
entered, before he was pushed away from the society of men
and hanged in the air, on a cross.

And then another desert, another non-literal desert: the
tomb. Like the desert, like the night, it is a symbol of negation.
As the desert is barren, neither fruitful like a garden, nor

populated like a city, as the night is dark, deprived of light, so the tomb is a place of absence, of negation, the place of death, a resting-place for a corpse. Desert – night – tomb: all conditions in which human activity is denied, cut off ('night comes,' says Jesus, 'when no one can work': John 9:4). Yet all places where God can work, where the divine power can be manifest: 'The Lord . . . will make her wilderness like Eden, her desert like the garden of the Lord' (Isa. 51:3). Or as we hear in the Paschal Proclamation on Easter night:

> This is the night, in which first you led our fathers, the children of Israel, out of Egypt and made them cross the Red Sea dry-foot.
>
> This is then the night, that purged the darkness of sin by the light of the pillar of fire.
>
> This is the night, which today throughout the world separates those who believe in Christ from the vices of the world and the obscurity of sin, restores them to grace, and joins them to holiness.
>
> This is the night, in which, having destroyed the chains of death, Christ rose from hell victorious.

This is the night, this is the night . . . when God acts. And so, in the resurrection, by God's power, the tomb becomes a place of life. So Orthodox Christians at Mattins of Holy Saturday sing such verses as these:

> O happy tomb! It received within itself the Creator, as one asleep, and it was made a divine treasury of life, for our salvation who sing: O God our Deliverer, blessed art Thou.
>
> The Life of all submits to be laid in the tomb, according to the law of the dead, and He makes it a source of awakening, for our salvation who sing: O God our Deliverer, blessed art Thou.[7]
>
> Come, let us see our Life lying in the tomb, that He may give life to those that in other tombs lie dead.[8]

In the chants for Holy Saturday the tomb of Christ becomes,

40

as it were, transparent to another symbol of profound negation: that of hell. In entering the tomb, Christ enters hell, the place of the dead, and frees all those whom death has held captive in hell, or Hades, beginning with Adam:

> Today hell groans and cries aloud: 'My dominion has been swallowed up; the Shepherd has been crucified and He has raised Adam. I am deprived of those whom once I ruled; in my strength I devoured them, but now I have cast them forth. He who was crucified has emptied the tombs; the power of death has no more strength.' Glory to Thy Cross, O Lord, and to Thy Resurrection.[9]

The desert – the night – the tomb – even hell itself: all symbols of negation and loss, but all capable of transformation by the power of God. The ways through the desert are ways that explore the limits of negation and loss and find beyond that evidence of the power of God, and resurrection. Symbols are reversed, or juxtaposed with startling contrariety: the narrow grave becomes the bridal bed, hell itself leads us back to paradise:

> Joseph asked for the body of Jesus and he laid it in his own new tomb: for it was fitting that the Lord should come forth from the grave as from a bridal chamber. O Thou who hast broken the power of death and opened the gates of Paradise to men, glory to Thee![10]

NOTES

1 Quoted by Mary Craig in her introd. to *God of the Impossible: daily readings with Carlo Carretto* (London, 1988), p. xii.
2 See A. M. Ramsey, *The Glory of God and the Transfiguration of Christ* (London, 1949), p. 113.
3 See, for example, Jean Daniélou, *From Glory to Glory* (London, 1962).
4 Quoted in Lucienne Portier, *Un précurseur: l'abbé Huvelin* (Paris, 1979), p. 162.
5 *Pensées*, no. 136 (Lafuma edn; Eng. tr. A. J. Krailsheimer, Harmondsworth, 1966, p. 67.)

6 Quoted in Portier, pp. 172 f.
7 *The Lenten Triodion*, tr. Mother Mary and Archimandrite Kallistos Ware (London, 1970), p. 650.
8 ibid. p. 652.
9 ibid. pp. 655 f.
10 ibid. p. 652.

3

The Desert Fathers

The desert does not figure prominently in the earliest history of the Church. True, St Paul, after his conversion, did not, according to his own account, straight away begin to preach the gospel but withdrew into the desert of Arabia (Gal. 1:17); and St John was exiled to the island of Patmos – a deserted island makes a very effective desert – and there received the series of revelations that form the final book of the Bible. But these would seem to be isolated examples. Christianity seems to have spread, first of all, in the cities of the Mediterranean world. But the early Christians did not feel themselves to be at home in that world. The paganism of Graeco-Roman society was very much a religion that suffused the whole of life, so that to be a Christian was to be excluded in many ways from the surrounding society. They faced, too, the constant threat of persecution, though it was sporadic rather than systematic. Christians applied to themselves the terms used to describe resident aliens: *paroikoi, xenoi* in Greek, *peregrini* in Latin. Here they were not at home, here they were aliens. They identified themselves with the great heroes of faith of the Old Testament who 'acknowledged that they were strangers and exiles on the earth' (Heb. 11:13): they were those who 'desire a better country, that is, a heavenly one. Therefore God is not ashamed to be called their God, for he has prepared for them a city' (Heb. 11:16). So St Paul, in the letter to the Ephesians, takes for granted that *here* Christians are aliens, when he says, 'you are no longer strangers and sojourners, but you are fellow citizens with the saints and members of the household of God' (Eph. 2:19): for Christians, their 'commonwealth is in heaven' (Phil. 3:20).

This idea, that the world is for Christians, if not a desert, at any rate not their homeland but a foreign country, penetrated deeply into the early Christian consciousness. The letter from the Church of Rome to the Church of Corinth, written at the end of the first century and usually called the First Letter of Clement, begins: 'From the Church of God temporarily resident in Rome to the Church of God temporarily resident in Corinth . . .' ('temporarily resident' translates the Greek *paroikein*). Other letters from one church to another follow the same pattern. In the second century an anonymous letter written to a Roman official called Diognetus describes the presence of Christians in the world in these terms:

> Though they are residents at home in their own countries, their behaviour there is more like that of aliens (*paroikoi*); they take their full part as citizens, but they also submit to everything as if they were foreigners (*xenoi*). For them, any foreign country is a motherland, and any motherland is a foreign country. (*To Diog.* 5.5)

And yet, the anonymous apologist insists, it is these foreigners who are the leaven in the lump of society: or, to use his own analogy:

> the relation of Christians to the world is that of a soul to the body . . . The soul, shut inside the body, nevertheless holds the body together; and though they are confined within the world as in a dungeon, it is Christians who hold the world together. The soul, which is immortal, must dwell in a mortal tabernacle; and Christians, as they sojourn for a while (*paroikousin*) among corruptible things, look for incorruptibility in the heavens. (ibid. 6.1, 7 f)

Our author uses the traditional notion of the contrast, even antagonism, between soul and body, spirit and flesh, to explain the persecution of Christians by the world, and indeed (with slightly grim humour) remarks that just as hardship is good for the soul, so persecution is good for Christians: they thrive on it. Martyrdom, for the early Church, was a beginning, not an end: the martyr woke up in kingdom of heaven, his death was his heavenly birthday.[1]

It is then perhaps not surprising that the call of the desert only begins to be heard as something distinct when Christians begin to feel themselves at home in the world: in some places already during the third century (Origen bears witness to this: see *Against Celsus* 3.9),[2] and generally throughout the Roman Empire after the Emperor Constantine embraced Christianity and began to favour the Church. The language of the Church 'temporarily resident' became merely conventional: *paroikia* is the word used for the territory governed by a bishop, a diocese we would say (it is the word from which our 'parish' derives). As Christians found themselves increasingly at home in the world, so the call of the desert became audible, at first for a few, later on for many.

One of the first to hear the call of the desert was an Egyptian peasant who came to be known as Antony the Great. After his death, at the age of more than a hundred, in 356, his life was written – the first of many saints' lives – probably in Coptic (the ordinary spoken language of Egypt) by a disciple: but the version that became well known was the Greek version, in which the great bishop of Alexandria, St Athanasius, who also thought of himself as a disciple of the great ascetic, almost certainly had a hand.[3] According to this life Antony was the son of well-to-do Christian parents. When he was in his late teens his parents died, leaving him with a much younger sister. One day he heard read in church Jesus' words to the rich young man, 'If you want to be perfect, go and sell all that you possess and give to the poor, and come and follow me' (Matt. 19:21). He felt that they were addressed directly to him and went and sold all his property and gave the proceeds to the poor. He placed his sister with the community of virgins attached to his local church (she later became their leader), and went to sit at the feet of an old man in the next village who had spent his life in solitary prayer. Gradually Antony withdrew further and further from the villages of his youth. First he went to live in tombs that were situated (as all cemeteries were in antiquity) outside the villages; then he sought the desert itself, first of all his so-called 'Outer Mountain', at Pispir on the east bank of the

Nile, about fifty miles south of Memphis, where he lived in solitude in a deserted fort for twenty years. As he lived there 'never going out and seldom seen by others', he attracted great renown: many wanted to follow his example and learn from him. At last they broke down the door of the fort, and

> Antony came forth as out of a shrine, as one initiated into sacred mysteries and filled with the Spirit of God . . . When they saw him, they were astonished to see that his body had kept its former appearance, that it was neither obese from want of exercise, not emaciated from his fastings and struggles with the demons . . . The state of his soul was pure . . . all balanced, as one governed by reason and standing in his natural state. (*Life* 14).[4]

By this time Antony was about fifty-five: we are now in the first decade of the fourth century, the period of the Great Persecution instigated by the Emperor Diocletian. Antony and his monks went publicly to Alexandria to support those who were suffering persecution, but though Antony is said to have longed for martyrdom, he was denied this and became what the *Life* calls a 'daily martyr in his conscience, ever fighting the battles of the Faith' (*Life* 47). During this period many flocked to Antony, to seek his advice as a holy man or to seek to pursue the ascetic life under his guidance. Eventually Antony withdrew yet more deeply into the desert, to his 'Inner Mountain', Mount Colzim (now called St Antony's Mount), much further – three days' journey – over towards the Red Sea, about 100 miles south-east of present-day Cairo. 'At the base of the mountain there was water, crystal-clear, sweet, and very cold. Spreading out from there was flat land and a few scraggy date-palms. Antony . . . fell in love with the place' (*Life* 49 f). Antony spent the rest of his life, sometimes on the Inner Mountain, sometimes visiting his Outer Mountain where other monks lived and where people from the 'world' came to visit him.

That bare account of Antony's life brings out, not just the importance of the desert in his life, but something of the meaning the desert had for him. Take first the description of his appearance after twenty years' solitude on the Outer

Mountain: Antony appears in his 'natural' state, in the form of perfect manhood, maintaining a perfect balance between the contrary 'unnatural' extremes that the human form can take. More precisely one can say that there is glimpsed in Antony the natural state of man, as God intended it, in paradise, in the Garden of Eden. The desert, for Antony, has become a way to paradise, to the lost state of harmony and perfection. And so Antony is described as 'falling in love' with the Inner Mountain: the desert, in its simplicity and austerity, is a place of beauty. Charles Kingsley described it in these terms:

> The eastward view from Antony's old home must be one of the most glorious in the world, save for the want of verdure and of life. For Antony, as he looked across the Gulf of Akaba, across which, far above, the Israelites had passed in old times, could see the sacred peaks of Sinai, flaming against the blue sky with that intensity of hue which is scarcely exaggerated, it is said, by the bright scarlet colour in which Sinai is always painted in medieval illuminations.[5]

The description of Antony's attainment of the natural, paradisal state of man is paralleled in the accounts of the sufferings of the martyrs. Pionius' body appears after he has been burnt alive in Smyrna 'like that of an athlete in full array at the height of his powers . . . his face shone once again – wondrous grace!'[6] In the account of the martyrdom of St Perpetua and her companions the visions she records often return to the idea of their re-entering a garden:

> Then I saw an immense garden, and in it a grey-haired man sat in shepherd's garb; tall he was, and milking sheep. And standing around him were many thousands of people clad in white garments. He raised his head, looked at me, and said: 'I am glad you have come, my child' . . .

> While we were being carried by these four angels, a great open space appeared, which seemed to be a garden, with rose bushes and all manner of trees. The trees were as tall

as cypresses, and their leaves were constantly falling. In the garden there were four other angels more splendid than the others. When they saw us they paid us homage and said to the other angels in admiration: 'Why, here they are! Here they are!'⁷

The martyrs are going home, home to paradise, home to human life in harmony with God as God had intended it, a spiritual harmony that pervades their bodies, so that their beauty is manifest, their faces are radiant. Antony's way to paradise was the desert: the experience of the desert restored his body to its natural harmony and his face was so radiant that those who visited him recognized him immediately 'as if drawn by his eyes ... The joy in his soul expressed itself in the cheerfulness of his face ...' (*Life* 67). Antony was denied literal martyrdom for the sake of Christ: in his cell, in the desert, he became 'a daily martyr in his conscience'.

There is another parallel between the monk, as typified by Antony, and the martyr, brought out in the way each of them is seen as an athlete, engaged in competitive struggle (*agōn*). This struggle is a struggle to gain self-mastery and thus to fight against the enemies of Christ. With St Paul, both the martyr and the monk could say, 'For we are not contending against flesh and blood, but against the principalities, against the powers, against the world rulers of this present darkness, against the spiritual hosts of wickedness in the heavenly places' (Eph. 6:12). Perpetua dreamt of her coming encounter with the wild beasts in the arena. In her dreams she is victorious. When she wakes up she realizes 'that it was not with wild beasts that I would fight but with the Devil, but I knew that I would win the victory'.⁸ The *Life of St Antony* – and the stories of the Desert Fathers generally – is full of accounts of struggles with demons. This explains something of the attraction of the desert, and the fact that Antony saw the tombs as a stepping-stone to the desert: in both cases he was seeking out the demons. The tombs, the place of the dead, are naturally 'haunted', a natural place for supernatural malevolence, for the demons. And the desert too, the solitude of the desert, is a place where demons are to be encountered *par excellence*.

The ancient world readily believed in supernatural beings – not as exalted as gods, but more exalted than human beings – in terms of which much that was beyond the scope of human explanation, both in the natural realm and in terms of relationships between human beings and indeed in the inner anxieties of the heart, could be explained. The Greeks called them *daimones* – they could be good or bad; the Hebrews called them angels – again, good or bad. But the whole paraphernalia of polytheism was regarded by Christians as wicked and corrupt, and so the agents used to explain the workings of prayer, sacrifice, divination and clairvoyance in Graeco-Roman paganism were readily regarded as malevolent, with the result that *daimon* came eventually to have a wholly negative connotation for Christians: a *daimon* was a malevolent supernatural being (the only meaning of the more usual English transliteration: demon). Demons were slanderous, deceitful agents opposed to the true God, and to Jesus Christ, the revelation of the true God. Those who sought the Truth, nakedly, for its own sake, were the objects of the onslaughts of these demons, these deceivers. It is a struggle between Truth for its own sake and comforting lies, and often waged in a very down-to-earth way: as, for instance, when Antony decides to set out for the desert:

> But there was the Enemy again! Seeing his earnestness and wishing to thwart it, he projected the illusion of a large disc of silver into the road. But Antony, seeing through the trickery of the Hater of Goodness, stopped, and, looking at the disc, exposed the Devil in it, saying: 'A disc in the desert? Where does that come from? This is not a travelled highway, and there is no track of any people coming this way ... This is a trick of the Devil. You will not thwart my resolution by this, Devil. Let this thing perish with you.' As Antony said this, it disappeared like smoke leaving fire. (*Life* 11)

Here Antony exposes the deceit of the devil by thought, by reason. Often enough calm, objective reason (which naturally leads to the truth and is only misled by partiality) is enough to combat the demons. But not always: they are crafty, the demons, superhumanly so, and can only be overthrown by Christ, ultimately by Christ's victory on the cross. Hence the importance of the sign of the cross, the sign of Christ's victory, for St Antony. But Christ's victory on the cross is something that each of us must make his own: it promises that sin and wickedness are not invincible, and encourages us to struggle in the conviction that evil can be overcome. This is brought out in the account of Antony's struggle with the demons that occurred in the tombs before he set out for the desert: the temptation in which the demons appear in the forms of all sorts of threatening and loathsome animals – the episode that inspired many painters, as well as the final scene of Flaubert's *La Tentation de Saint Antoine*. At the end of his struggle, Antony

> looked up and saw as it were the roof opening and a beam of light coming down to him. The demons suddenly were gone and the pain in his body ceased at once and the building was restored to its former condition. Antony, perceiving that help had come, breathed more freely and felt relieved of his pains. And he asked the vision: 'Where were you? Why did you not appear at the beginning to stop my pains?' And a voice came to him: 'Antony, I was here, but I waited to see your struggle. And now, because you held out and did not surrender, I will ever be your helper and I will make you renowned everywhere.' (*Life* 10)

The very readiness of the ancient world to believe in angels and demons poses a problem for us. Perhaps such beings are merely part of their world-view, part of an apparatus of explanation that has been superseded by all that has been discovered since, something that can – and even should – be readily 'demythologized'. Even if we do not go as far as that, we may well think there are more important things to seek to understand than demons: Karl Barth, in his *Church Dogmatics*, has a lengthy section on angelology, but even he allows the demons no more than a 'short, sharp glance'.[9] However, perhaps for our purposes – understanding the place of the desert in the world of the early ascetics – we can sidestep any fundamental questions about the nature of demons, without evading what the demons stood for in the experience of the Desert Fathers.

For much of the desert tradition, two words are almost synonymous: *logismos* and demon. *Logismos* means a 'thought', and the *logismoi* we encounter in the writings of the Desert Fathers are thoughts caused by demons. But 'thought' is a feeble word and conveys little of the real meaning of *logismos* here. Peter Brown captures the real thrust of *logismos* when he says:

> Consent to evil thoughts, many of which were occasioned, in the first instance, by the dull creakings of the body – by its need for food and its organic, sexual drives – implied a decision to collaborate with other invisible spirits, the demons, whose pervasive presence, close to the human person, was registered in the 'heart' in the form of inappropriate images, fantasies, and obsessions. For these demonic promptings also had a dynamism that could not be explained by the normal stream of conscious thought. Hence . . . the 'heart' was a place where momentous, faceless options were mercifully condensed in the form of conscious trains of thought – *logismoi*. Little wonder, then, that the wise Solomon had said: *Keep thy heart with all diligence.* For to consent to such *logismoi* was to 'consecrate oneself' to demonic partners. It was to give oneself over, on many more levels of the self than the conscious person, to an alternative identity: it was to lose oneself to the powers of numbness that still lurked in the hidden reaches of the universe, and to take on the character of chill demonic spirits who had been content to exist without the ardent search for God.[10]

Logismoi were not thoughts in the sense of 'ideas', but trains of thought, strings of considerations, that invaded the heart, occluded it, divided it, and destroyed any chance of a single-hearted devotion to, search for, God. The demons inspired such *logismoi*, they lay behind them as behind so many idols, inviting the kind of total surrender that is due only to God.

Demons belong to the desert, to the solitude of the desert. Evagrius says that away from the desert, in cities and villages,

51

and even in monastic communities, the demons attack indirectly, through other people, through the annoyances they cause and the tensions created by living together, but in the desert the demons attack the hermit directly, hand-to-hand.[11] It is only when one is alone, deep in solitude, that one enters into oneself sufficiently profoundly to discover how far one is from singleness of heart, that one discovers within oneself any deep longing for God. Getting on in the world clutters up the heart, and assuages its deep longing for God with passing satisfactions. A common image of the aim of the solitude of the desert is that of leaving a bowl of water still, so that at last the surface of the water is undisturbed, and one can see one's face in it.[12] In that solitude, *logismoi* are like ripples that disturb the surface of the water, or cracks that let the world in and destroy the reality of the desert. Evagrius classified these *logismoi* into eight types – eight cracks in the heart, as it were, that can split the heart and rob one of single-minded devotion to God. These eight types of *logismoi* (or eight *logismoi*) are: gluttony, avarice, fornication, anger, grief, accidie (= listlessness), vainglory and pride. In this list we can see the origins of the seven deadly sins of the western Middle Ages, but there is an important difference: the seven deadly sins are a classification of sinful deeds, the eight *logismoi* are eight *temptations*, and their purpose is diagnostic. The temptations are not directly temptations to commit some grossly sinful act, they are rather temptations – distracting, discouraging trains of thought – that play on the various weaknesses of human nature. The *logismos* of gluttony, for instance, is rarely a matter of visions of, or longing for, some splendid banquet: it is rather a matter of worries lest the extremely austere diet of the hermit undermine his health, and what is wrong with that is that the hermit is letting his worries distract him from his search for God.

Put another way, the *logismoi* can be seen as hindrances to *prayer*. These hindrances take, roughly, three forms: they can distract, they can occlude, and they can turn the ascetic in on himself in a way that destroys the very nature of prayer. Anyone who has ever tried to pray silently for any length of time knows about distraction. Praying silently seems like doing nothing, and our busy minds will not be quiet, but ceaselessly start off on one train of thought or another. Even if one manages to be quiet for a few moments, one's mind starts off on a train of thought about how spiritual one has become, how successfully one can pray! It is not difficult to imagine how greatly distraction can be magnified, if one is keeping silent not just for twenty minutes but for hours at a time. Distractions are usually seen as remnants of the world the hermit has left behind: time and the self-denial and austerity of life in the desert will itself weaken these distractions . . . gradually. Time, and the perseverance it needs, will test and prove the commitment of the hermit. That is the long-term solution, and it is no more than a reassertion of the aim of the desert life: escape from distraction comes, as one comes closer to single-hearted prayer to God. It is summed up in one of Abba Arsenius' 'words': 'Strive with all your might to bring your interior activity into accord with God, and you will overcome exterior passions' (Arsenius, 9).[13] Or in Evagrius' treatise *On Prayer*: ' "Go, sell what you have and give to the poor; take up your cross" and deny yourself. That is how you will be able to pray without distraction.'[14] That is the long-term solution: undisturbed prayer is what the hermit is aiming for, and there is never any suggestion that such prayer is anything other than the fruit of a long struggle and much perseverance.

But distractions do not actually prevent one from praying. Distractions can be met by short prayers for help: 'And if the conflict grows fiercer say, "Lord, help!" He knows very well what we need and shows his mercy' (Marcarius the Great, 19); and in that way distractions impel the monk to dependence on God's mercy; they keep alive within him a sense of repentance. *Logismoi* that occlude prayer are more serious: these darken the mind and cause ruin to the state of prayer.[15] The soul afflicted by such *logismoi* can no longer pray at all. The *logismoi* that occlude prayer are those inspired by anger, resentment, brooding on slights (or imagined slights) to oneself. 'People who hoard their miseries and brood on their wrongs and then expect to pray are like people who draw water and pour it into a jug with holes in it,' says Evagrius.[16] Here the fundamental remedy is the realization that anger directed against other people is never justified:

When you pray as you should, you will run into things of a kind to make you suppose that it would be entirely right for you to make use of anger. But there is no such thing as justified anger against your neighbour. If you look, you will find that it is possible for the matter to be settled quite well without anger. Use any device you can to avoid losing your temper.[17]

To rise above such *logismoi*, no longer to be afflicted by them, is to attain the state that is usually described by the much-misunderstood word *apatheia*, which invites the translation 'passionlessness'. This suggests a state of numbness, insensitivity, and though such language is sometimes used to describe it, it conveys in modern English quite the wrong impression. *Apatheia* means a state of self-mastery and attention from which one cannot be dislodged by distractions or by the kind of outbursts of spiritual energy that expresses itself in anger and resentment. It is not a state of insensitivity: on the contrary it is a state of great sensitivity. But it is not the kind of sensitivity in which one is rendered ineffective by being constantly drawn hither and thither by impressions from without, rather it is the kind of sensitivity that is a form of *attention*. To attain this state is, however, to run a further risk, the risk summed up by the *logismoi*, the temptations, of vainglory and pride. If the monk begins to think that his state of *apatheia* constitutes some kind of a success, then he is open to vainglory: 'it is difficult to escape from the *logismos* of vainglory, because whatever you do to eliminate it becomes the occasion of fresh vainglory'.[18] Vainglory fills the monk with a sense of his spiritual importance and (Evagrius suggests) leads him to see visions, and to imagine that in these visions he is coming to see God who is invisible and unknowable, and thus the monk is deceived and falls into the power of the deceiver, the Devil.

The various collections of the sayings of the Desert Fathers provide a source of the practical wisdom based on the experience of the ascetics. They are not intended to be read systematically, rather their variety and their pithy, gnomic form are intended to provide many different points of contact with the very varied experience of humankind. Some sayings will strike home to one person, some to another; some will seem directed to my condition now, some will only become relevant later on. But certain themes run through the sayings as a whole: themes like the importance of prayer and stillness, of perseverance, of the cell, of penitence and obedience. By looking at some of these, we can form a more precise picture of the meaning of the desert for those whom we call *par excellence* the Desert Fathers.

Take the cell, for instance. This was the place where the monk lived and prayed. For hermits like Antony the cell would be isolated, beyond sight or sound of anyone. At the other extreme the cells would be rooms in a house where each monk slept and prayed: but otherwise they would eat, work and celebrate the monastic offices together. This pattern of *coenobitic* monasticism (from the Greek for 'common life') was first established by Pachomius (*c.* 290–346) in cultivated land, close to the Nile and not strictly desert at all (the precise location of his original foundation at Tabennesis is unknown). In between Antony's strict solitude and the communal monasticism of Pachomius, there was the semi-eremitical way established by St Ammon in Nitria and St Macarius in Scetis, where several monks lived in separate cells grouped together at a distance from one another and pursued a mainly solitary existence, coming together at the weekend to celebrate the Eucharist (such semi-eremitical arrangements were called *lavras* or, later, *sketes*). The cell was the monk's place in the desert: it was 'his' desert. 'Go, sit in your cell, and your cell will teach you everything' (Moses, 6). In the cell the monk was to pray, to work at some simple, undistracting task (like basket-making), and eat and sleep (sparingly). So Abba Poemen states:

> Living in your cell clearly means manual work, eating only once a day, silence, meditation; but really making progress in the cell means to experience contempt for yourself wherever you go, not to neglect the hours of prayer and to pray secretly. If you happen to have time without manual work, take up prayer and do it without disquiet. (Poemen, 168)

It is certainly intended to be dull so that distractions subside,

and the monk can concentrate on prayer, and begin to fulfil
St Paul's command to 'pray without ceasing' (1 Thess. 5:17).
What form did this prayer take? It was certainly out of the
experience of the monks that the daily cycle of prayer, later
called the divine office, took shape: mattins and lauds in the
night and early morning, short services at the first hour (that
is, one hour after sunrise, calculated as a twelfth of the (vari-
able) period of daylight), the third hour, the sixth hour
(noon), and the ninth hour (usually known in English as
prime, terce, sext and none), vespers towards sunset, and
compline before retiring to bed. These 'hours' do not seem to
have been part of the Egyptian practice, but they were certainly part of the Palestinian pattern.[19] We hear a lot about
short prayers, like the prayer of the publican: 'Lord, have
mercy on me, a sinner' (Luke 18:13). The use of such short
prayers, as a way of focusing attention on God and combating
distraction, in the East eventually developed into the Jesus
Prayer ('Lord Jesus Christ, Son of God, have mercy upon
me, a sinner').[20] But we also hear of recitation of the psalter
(which monks were expected to know by heart), not just as
part of the divine office, but as a way of praying on one's
own. On the place of the Psalms in the prayer of the hermit,
Roland Walls has said:

> The staple offering of praise, thanksgiving, penitence and
> petition takes the same form as that of the universal
> Church, of Israel, of Christ Himself. Alone, but never
> alone, the hermit joins all suffering, sinful, despairing, as
> well as happy, humanity in articulating its unsaid prayer.
> He is, through his solitude, united to the praying Church
> through the praying Christ. It is the Psalter more than
> anything else that has preserved the essentially corporate
> and communal aspect of the Christian solitary and pre-
> vented him from escaping into a life abysmally concerned
> with soul culture, or losing his identity among undifferen-
> tiated contemplatives of all religions.[21]

The emphasis on remaining in one's cell raises acutely a
problem that affects the whole desert ideal: is not the pursuit
of solitude a kind of selfish indulgence? There are, for

instance, stories of a monk's resisting the temptation to go and visit a sick brother. Does not such an ideal militate against love for one's neighbour, the command to love that is the very heart of Christianity? It is important to raise this issue, as around it clusters a whole host of misconceptions. Would it, for instance, be an act of love to go and visit a sick brother, because one was bored with the cell and wanted a bit of a change? Love is a matter of giving, at the very least the giving of attention. But to go and see another as a distraction, is to go to fulfil a need; and though in giving we receive (often more than we have given), the reverse is not true.[22] First of all, at least, there is raised the question of the motive, the intention. And to raise it is important, even if we are not ourselves solitaries: out-going activity is not necessarily loving, it depends on the motive, one can only go out in love from an inwardness that is capable of stillness, of attention, of hearing and perceiving the other's need. But there is a deeper answer, which is already broached in the quotation from Roland Walls. The hermit is not alone for his own sake, and in entering, in stillness, into the heart and coming to know its waywardness, its capacity for evil and self-deception, the hermit enters – not from outside, but from within – into the broken condition of all humanity. And in his stillness he holds the whole of humanity close to the healing presence of God.

In another way too the desert is turned back towards the world it has turned away from. The original context of many of the sayings of the Desert Fathers is the seeking from those ascetics of help, advice, direction. Men (and women) visited the fathers of the desert to 'seek a word'. 'Father, give me a word': that is a phrase we often come across. The seeking of a word, and the giving of a word, though in some ways not unlike the seeking of messages from oracles that had formed an important part of pagan religious practice, had nothing magical about it: it is rather based on the unity of all men in Christ, a unity achieved by Christ's triumph over the evil that separates us one from another. The fathers of the desert, who lived close to Christ and in their struggles had participated in his victory, experienced this common humanity in Christ, and often knew the problems and anxieties of those who sought them out in a way that seems like clairvoyance. In some stories, their insight picks out a problem that the one seeking them was unaware of himself. Such a source of wisdom and insight, that could only be drawn on by those humble enough to seek it, was a precious gift from the desert to the world. As the French poet Edmond Jabès has said, 'the desert lends to the least gesture, to the most insignificant word, a slow rhythm of beyond-silence, beyond-life'.[23] It was a wisdom characterized by a gentle common sense, and a profound trust in God. Out of this experience the notion of spiritual fatherhood was born: something that has been preserved in both eastern and western Christianity to the present day.

It was a spiritual fatherhood born of spiritual fatherhood, for none of the Desert Fathers found their way in the desert without seeking the help of those who had tried to live the life before them. Even in the *Life of St Antony* it is stressed how Antony first sought the fruits of the experience of many older ascetics before he himself ventured into his own deeper solitude of the desert. And the later tradition is full of notable examples of spiritual fatherhood. An enormous collection of questions and answers survives from the sixth-century Gaza desert, where two old men, Varsanuphios and John – the Great Old Man and the Other Old Man – lived in complete seclusion in the vicinity of a monastery. Their advice was sought by many – by the monks of the monastery and by others from further afield – and, as they did not emerge from their cells, both the questions and their answers had to be written down: these bits of paper were preserved and eventually collected together. One of their disciples, Dorotheus, himself became an abbot and the writer of spiritual homilies: according to him, 'The Fathers say that to sit in one's cell is half, to visit the old men is the other half.'[24] Obedience to one's spiritual father was paramount: some of the stories seem quite absurd. For instance, there is the story told of John the Dwarf. His abba (Amoe) took a piece of wood and told him to water it. He had to go so far to fetch the water that he left in the evening and only returned the next morning. After three years the wood came to life and bore fruit. Abba Amoe took some of the fruit and carried it to the church, saying to the brothers, 'Take and eat of the fruit of obedience' (cf. John, 1). But the point of obedience was the submission of one's own will, so that that will could become totally open to God. Obedience implied humility and trust, and these are the foundation of the desert life.

The spiritual fatherhood of the desert was intended to create a new humanity, a humanity open to God and through which God's power could be felt. 'The desert became a city,' said St Athanasius in his *Life of St Antony* (14). He primarily meant that the desert became full of people, but a deeper meaning lies there: the desert became a city, *the* city, a foreshadowing of the city of God, a city bound together, not by human regulations but by a 'bearing of one another's burdens' (cf. Gal. 6:2), through which the redeemed humanity, brought into existence by Christ, could be realized. And that experience of humanity was for the sake of all humanity – for everyone who is our neighbour. So, despite the apparent flight from human society implied by the seeking out of the desert, John the Dwarf could say, 'The foundation is our neighbour' (John, 39), echoing the saying of St Antony's: 'Our life and our death are with our neighbour' (Antony, 9). In this way, as Evagrius put it, the monk, the solitary, is 'separated from all and united with all'.[25]

NOTES

The standard book in English on early monasticism is Derwas Chitty, *The Desert a City* (Oxford, 1966). See also, as well as the books cited in the notes, Helen Waddell, *The Desert Fathers* (London, 1936), which contains translations from the Latin versions of the traditions about the fathers of the desert; and Jean Gribomont OSB's distillation of much learning in *Christian Spirituality*, vol. I, ed. B. McGinn, J. Meyendorff and J. Leclercq OSB (London, 1986), pp. 86–112.

1   cf. *Martyrdom of Polycarp* 18.3. For the writings of the so-called 'apostolic fathers' quoted in this paragraph see *Early Christian Writings*, tr. M. Staniforth, new edn by A. Louth (Penguin Classics, 1987).
2   Where Origen speaks of 'the present time . . . when on account

of the multitude of people coming to the faith even rich men and persons in positions of honour, and ladies of high birth, favourably regard adherents of the faith': Origen, *Contra Celsum*, tr. and ed. H. Chadwick (Cambridge, 1953), p. 134.

3 See Andrew Louth, 'St Athanasius and the Greek *Life of Antony*' in *Journal of Theological Studies*, n.s. 39 (1988), pp. 504–9.

4 Quotations from *Athanasius: The Life of St Antony*, tr. R. T. Meyer (Ancient Christian Writers, 10; 1950).

5 Charles Kingsley, *The Hermits* (London, 1868), p. 128; quoted in Meyer, p. 6.

6 *Martyrdom of Pionius* 22: H. Musurillo (ed.), *Acts of the Christian Martyrs* (Oxford, 1972), p. 165.

7 *Martyrdom of SS Perpetua and Felicitas* 4, 11; Musurillo, pp. 111, 121.

8 ibid. 10; Musurillo, p. 119.

9 Karl Barth, *Kirchliche Dogmatik* III. 3 (Zürich, 1950), p. 609 (Eng. tr., Edinburgh, 1961; p. 519).

10 Peter Brown, *The Body and Society* (London, 1989), p. 167.

11 *Praktikos* 5; ed. A. and C. Guillaumont, vol. 2 (Sources Chrétiennes, 171), pp. 504 f.

12 See, for example, Saying 2 in *The Wisdom of the Desert Fathers*, tr. Sister Benedicta Ward SLG (Fairacres Publications, 48; 1975), p. 1.

13 Quotations from the Desert Fathers are taken from *The Sayings of the Desert Fathers*, tr. Ward.

14 *On Prayer* 17; tr. from: Evagrius: *Praktikos* and *On Prayer*, Dionysius the Areopagite: *Mystical Theology*, tr. Simon Tugwell OP (Oxford, 1987), p. 31.

15 Evagrius, *On Prayer* 27.

16 ibid. 22 (tr. Tugwell, p. 32).

17 ibid. 24 (Tugwell, ibid.).

18 *Praktikos* 30.

19 See Chitty, *The Desert a City*, p. 72.

20 On the Jesus Prayer, see Archimandrite (now Bishop) Kallistos Ware, *The Power of the Name* (Fairacres Publications, 43; rev. edn, 1977) and, for the history of the Jesus Prayer, his contributions to *The Study of Spirituality*, ed. C. P. M. Jones, G. Wainwright and E. J. Yarnold SJ (London, 1986), pp. 175–84. 242–58, and the literature cited in these articles.

21 In *Solitude and Communion*, ed. A. M. Allchin (Fairacres Publications, 66; 1977), pp. 52 f.

22 cf. Simone Weil on the effect of necessity on love in *Waiting for God* (London, 1951), pp. 132 f.

23 Quoted by Michael Edwards in a review in *Times Literary Supplement* (29 December 1989–4 January 1990), no. 4526, p. 1444.
24 In the edition of Dorotheus' spiritual works by L. Regnault OSB and J. de Préville OSB (Sources Chrétiennes, 92; 1963), p. 488. The correspondence of Varsanuphios and John has been translated into French by Regnault and P. Lemaire, with B. Outtier (Solesmes, 1972).
25 Evagrius, *On Prayer* 124.

4

Medieval Anchorism and Julian of Norwich

The desert is far from the city, and those who sought out the desert intended to distance themselves from immediate human affairs. Many of them must have succeeded all too well: the material recorded in the *Sayings of the Desert Fathers*, for instance, amounts to a series of disconnected snap-shots and only concerns several dozen of the fathers of the desert, whereas contemporary estimates talk of several thousand, which, even if exaggerated, must reflect a very large number.[1] The deserts of Palestine and Syria continued to attract devotees; localized 'deserts' grew up, islands and inaccessible peninsulas – notably in the high Byzantine period the island of Patmos and the peninsula called the Holy Mountain of Athos – where men lived out the various patterns of monasticism first explored in the Egyptian desert, away from the towns and cities of normal human life.

In the western Middle Ages the desert call continued to be heard: western Europe was a much bigger and wilder place than that we know today as the countries that make up the Common Market. Many monastic settlements were remote: on islands off the coast of France (like Lérins, where Honoratus founded a monastery in the fifth century), or barren headlands (like the Abbey of St Gildas where, much later, Abélard spent unhappy years). Among the Irish the desert ideal took another form, much closer to the early Christian experience of being exiles in this world: this was the ideal of perpetual wandering or pilgrimage. The Irish monks left their native lands and lived their lives as aliens – in England, on the continent – travelling, never settling down anywhere, never having a place this side of heaven to call their own.[2] In the

Cistercian reform the monks sought out remote, desolate places in which to build their monasteries. Even England, which seems too small and compact nowadays for anywhere to be really remote, had its 'deserts': the borders of England and Wales, the north of England stretching up towards Scotland, were isolated and barren areas. Here the Cistercians found 'deserts' for their monasteries: most famously Tintern (in the Wye valley), Fountains (in the Yorkshire dales), Rievaulx (in the North York moors). Various medieval monastic reforms sought to rediscover the solitary aspect of the desert: the reforms of Camaldoli and the Great Charterhouse, the latter of which was particularly influential in England. England also knew, to a degree more pronounced than elsewhere, the quest for the desert in the strict enclosure of the hermit's cell or anchorage.[3] Two of the great names of the remarkable flowering of mystical literature of the fourteenth century – Richard Rolle and Julian of Norwich – certainly spent part of their lives as hermits, Richard finally at Hampole in Yorkshire, and Julian in her anchorhold in Norwich, and the same may be true of the other great mystical writers of that time: the author of *The Cloud of Unknowing* and Walter Hilton. Richard Rolle came from Yorkshire, and spent most of his life there: a Yorkshire which then must have been very much a wild and inhospitable desert – as such it had attracted the Cistercians in such numbers in the twelfth century. Even today the moors, covered with gorse and heather, are wild and bleak, with grasslands more hospitable to sheep than to man. We know quite a bit about Rolle: he came from the southern edge of the North York moors, and spent time in the northern dales before settling at Hampole in the West Riding. But though Julian lived as a hermit in the busy city of Norwich, the 'desert' to which she withdrew seems to have protected her very effectively from human interest. She barely seems to graze the surface of the history of her time, while her influence 500 years later is enormous and seems to know no limits.[4]

It is perhaps worth emphasizing how completely Julian hid herself from the interest of her age. Apart from what can be gleaned from her writings, and that is little more than the events that accompanied her visions in 1373, together with the fact that at that time she was thirty and a half years old (even the precise date of the visions is not entirely certain, the manuscripts disagreeing between 8 and 13 – viii and xiii – May), the only certain evidence we have about her derives from the remark of the scribe who copied the so-called 'Short Text' of her Revelations, who says that in 1413 she was still alive and living in Norwich as an anchoress. (Julian's *Revelations* survive in two distinct versions: a 'Short Text' which is simply an account of the Revelations and the events surrounding them – presumably written down shortly afterwards – and a 'Long Text' which incorporates a great deal of theological reflection and, by its own account, must have been written at least twenty years after the revelations occurred.)[5] Almost all the other evidence about an anchoress called Julian at Norwich – some wills and the account in *The Book of Margery Kempe* about her visit to 'an anchoress . . . named Dame Jelyan'[6] – is rendered uncertain by the fact that Julian took her name from the church, St Julian's Conisford, to which her anchorhold was attached. If she did so, it is likely enough that any other anchoress living there would also have called herself Julian. However, the account of Margery Kempe's visit to Norwich is so close in date to 1413 when we know Julian was an anchoress in Norwich (Margery went to Norwich to seek counsel about a private vow of chastity she wished to take, a vow that was taken secretly by her and her husband on 23 June 1413), that it seems captious to doubt that the anchoress Julian whom Margery visited was any other than the author of the Revelations. It remains the case, however, that Margery does not identify her as such: she seems to know nothing of any fame attached to Dame Julian as a notable spiritual writer. And when we look at the manuscript evidence for Julian's Revelations, that seems hardly surprising. Seventeen manuscripts of *The Cloud of Unknowing* survive, twelve of them from the fifteenth century; over fifty manuscripts of Walter Hilton's *Ladder of Perfection* survive, and it was first printed by Wynkyn de Worde in 1494. Only one medieval manuscript contains a complete text of Julian's Revelations, and even then it is of the Short Text, tagged on, together with several other devotional texts, to a group of Richard Rolle's writings. The only other medieval manuscript containing Julian's words has a collection of short extracts from the Long Text of the Revelations. The principal manu-scripts containing the Long Text – one now in the Biblio-thèque Nationale in Paris, the other two now in the British Library in London – all belong to the seventeenth century. It is, then, hardly surprising that Margery Kempe knew nothing of Julian as a spiritual writer: few of her contemporar-ies seem to have valued her writings, they survive almost by chance.

Almost anything else we say about Julian's life as it impinged on the society of her day is speculation. We do not know when she became an anchoress at Norwich, nor when she died. We do not know what she did before she became an anchoress: whether she had been a nun, perhaps at Carrow which was the patron of the living of St Julian's Conisford, or whether she had lived as a laywoman, and perhaps mar-ried, had children and been widowed.[7] We do not know where she came from: she may have lived in or near Norwich all her life, but she may very well have come from somewhere else. (It has been argued from the language of the manuscript of the Short Text that she may have been a Yorkshirewoman, and this argument is supported by her reference to St John of Beverley, though the fact that Henry V ascribed the English victory at Agincourt in 1415 to his intercession suggests that his fame was not purely local.)[8] All we know about Julian's 'historical' life is that she was born in 1342 (probably in November), that she experienced a series of visions on 8 or 13 May 1373, when she was seriously ill and thought she was dying, that about fifteen years later, and again three months less than twenty years later (in February 1393), she received further insight into the meaning of her Revelations, that in 1413 she was a recluse in an anchorhold attached to the church of St Julian's Conisford, in Norwich, and that around that time she probably received a visit from Margery Kempe. By that time she would have been in her early seventies, a considerable age in the Middle Ages, but we have no idea how much longer she continued to live.

Julian's 'desert', then, provided a very effective retreat from the world of her day. Whether it was in her 'desert', while she was living as a recluse, or at some time before her enclosure at

St Julian's Church, that she received her visions (or even the two subsequent moments of enlightenment in 1388 and 1393), is something else that we do not know, but we do know that Julian did not see her visions as intended simply for herself: 'I am sure,' she says in the earlier Short Text, 'I saw it for the profit of many others.'[9] The manuscript evidence suggests that this conviction was frustrated in her own time: the growing popularity of her *Revelations* in various editions and selections in this century shows, however, that her conviction was not ultimately groundless. It is very strange to think, but unavoidable none the less, that the recluse who was almost totally hidden from the world of her own day has a message that has spoken to the hearts of many in this century, more than 500 years later. What was revealed to her was revealed in a way completely of her time – what could be more characteristic of the late Middle Ages than a series of visions in which the crucified Jesus appeared in all the freshly-perceived realism of his dying? – and yet, though wholly of her time, she speaks as a contemporary in ours. One recalls some words of David Jones about a work of art showing 'signs of being essentially of now, yet reaching back to "the foundation of the city", and [being] also, or rather, *therefore*, valid for the future'.[10] Julian's visions unquestionably show 'signs of being essentially of [the medieval] now' and 'yet reaching back to "the foundation of the city" ' are '*therefore*, valid for the future', which is our present.

What was her 'now'? What was her life as a recluse in fourteenth- and fifteenth-century England like?[11] (For whether or not she received her visions as a hermit, they were certainly a critical point in her life, as must have been her decision to become a hermit, and we can hardly imagine that one life could embrace two such decisive moments without their being related.) In the early thirteenth century a rule was written for anchoresses called variously in the manuscripts the *Ancrene Riwle* or the *Ancrene Wisse*: it enjoyed enormous influence and it is unlikely that Julian's experience of her anchorhold was untouched by the ideals and advice of this rule for anchoresses.

The *Ancrene Riwle* is divided into eight parts, and is mainly concerned – as one would expect – with building up the inner life of the anchoress.[12] The six inner sections are a long discussion of the inward life of struggle to which the anchoress is committed. Section 2 is concerned with the five senses, 'which guard the heart as watchmen when they are faithful'; section 3 compares the life of the anchoress to that on a bird, developed in the form of allegorical commentary of various scriptural verses, mainly from the Psalms; section 4 deals with the temptations of various kinds (divided up according to the seven chief sins: the lion of pride, the serpent of envy, the unicorn of wrath, the bear of sloth, the fox of covetousness, the swine of greediness, and the scorpion of lechery, each with its progeny – the bear of sloth, for instance, has these 'whelps': torpor, pusillanimity, dullness-of-heart, idleness, a grudging, grumbling heart, deadly sorrow, negligence, despair); section 5 is about confession; section 6 about penitence; section 7 about love and purity of heart. These sections are full of firm, but gentle teaching. The life of the anchoress is to be simple and austere, constantly drawn to the memory of God and devoted to prayer for the Church and the world. But the rule is opposed to any extremes of asceticism:

> Wear no iron, nor haircloth, nor hedgehog-skins; and do not beat yourselves therewith, nor with a scourge of leather thongs, nor leaded; and do not with holly nor with briars cause yourselves to bleed without leave of your confessor; and do not, at one time, use too many flagellations.[13]

The advice is wise and practical, and enlivened with deftly-sketched examples, and little flights of allegorical fancy. One of the birds to which the anchoress is compared is the owl, the 'night fowl':

> The night fowl in the eaves betokeneth recluses who dwell under the eaves of the church, that they may understand that they ought to be of so holy life that the whole holy church, that is, all Christian people, may learn and be supported upon them, and that they may bear her up with their holiness of life and their pious prayers. And an anchoress is for this reason called anchoress, and anchored under the church as an anchor under a ship, to hold the

ship so that neither waves nor storms may overwhelm it. In like manner shall anchoresses, or the anchor, hold the Holy Church Universal, which is called a ship, so firm, that the devil's storms, which are temptations, may not overwhelm it.[14]

Or again:

The night fowl flieth by night, and seeks his food in the darkness; and thus shall the recluse fly with contemplation, that is, with high and holy prayers, by night towards heaven, and seek during the night nourishment for her soul. In the night, the anchoress ought to be watchful and diligent about spiritual attainments; wherefore, there cometh immediately after, 'I have watched, and am even as it were a sparrow, that sitteth alone upon the house-top' (Ps. 101:8). I was watchful, saith David, in the character of an anchorite, and like a lonely sparrow under a roof. I was watchful: for this is the duty of an anchoress – to watch much.[15]

The imagery of the recluse as a night fowl draws attention to the importance of night time as a time of prayer and watching in the life of the anchoress. The first part of the *Ancrene Riwle* concerns the times and form of prayer. As one would expect, the heart of this is the ordered pattern of the divine office: the regular hours that we first find in the fourth century and that had been elaborated since. On getting-up – during the night in winter, or at daybreak in summer – the night office is said, then the hours throughout the day, vespers in the evening, and compline before going to bed. This structure forms a backbone, so to speak, around which is built other devotion: various offices in honour of our Lady, or on behalf of the departed, litanies and psalms, with rules about kneeling down (in adoration or penitence) and the use of various short prayers, said frequently (or repeatedly) by heart, as the anchoress gets dressed or prepares to say the various offices. Such prayers as: 'Jesus Christ, Son of the living God, have mercy upon us. Thou who didst condescend to be born of a virgin, have mercy on us' or:

We adore thee, O Christ, and we bless thee, who, by the holy cross, hast redeemed the world.

We adore thy cross, O Lord. We commemorate thy glorious passion.

Pity us, O thou who didst suffer for us.

Hail, O holy Cross, worthy tree, whose precious wood bore the treasure of the world!

Hail, O Cross, who in the body of Christ wast dedicated, and with limbs adorned, as with pearls.

O Cross, wood triumphant over the world. True safety, hail!

Among woods none such, for leaf, flower, bud.

O Christian medicine, heal, heal the sound and the sick.

The pattern of prayer laid down in the first part of the Rule provides a kind of rhythm of recollection and aspiration to accompany the life of the recluse. That life is to be lapped about by silence. The recluse's meals are to be eaten alone and in silence: there are to be opportunities for the recluse to talk to those who come to seek her counsel (as Margery sought the counsel of Dame Julian), but these are to be limited, and whole days to be set aside for complete silence: every Friday; in Advent and during Ember weeks Wednesdays and Fridays; during Lent three days; and the whole of Holy Week until noon on Easter eve, as well as the whole of every night from compline until after prime.

The final part of the *Ancrene Riwle* concerns various practical matters (which are also discussed, as occasion arises, in the body of the work). The cell of the recluse has windows. One opens on to the church, so that she may hear mass each day: various devotions are suggested in the first part for the recluse as she participates in mass from her cell:

after the kiss of peace in the mass, when the priest communicates,[16] forget there all the world, and there be entirely out of the body; there in glowing love embrace your blessed

69

Saviour who is come down from heaven into your breast's bower, and hold him fast until he shall have granted whatever you wish for.[17]

– though the recluse, as a laywoman, is only to receive communion fifteen times a year. Another window faces on to the parlour, and is covered with a black cloth with a white cross stitched on it, which is drawn back when the anchoress talks to her maid, or to visitors. Other practical matters include clothing – simple, but warm; diet – no flesh-meat, but neither are recluses to fast on bread and water; the manual work of the recluse – she is not to make purses or other rich things, but church vestments, and clothes for the poor. Much space is devoted to the recluse's servant or servants: as the recluse was not to leave her cell, she needed a servant to look after her, or two if one of them was needed to go and buy provisions from time to time. Recluses are not to keep domestic animals, 'except only a cat'.

The picture of the life of the anchoress that emerges from the *Ancrene Riwle* is probably close to the picture we should have of Julian's life as a recluse at St Julian's Church, Norwich (apart from obvious differences, the most notable being that the *Ancrene Riwle* envisages three recluses attached to a single church, whereas Julian seems to have been on her own). It was the life in which, perhaps, Julian's reflections on her visionary experience matured and took the shape found in the 'Long Text', or to which she was eventually led as she sought to be faithful to the vocation that her visionary experience had laid upon her.

It is probably best to think of these visions or 'showings' as a unity, and to call her account of them, with Marion Glasscoe, 'A Revelation of Love', rather than 'Revelations of Divine Love', as it has been known since Serenus Cressy first published them as *XVI Revelations of Divine Love* in 1670.[18] Julian herself seems to have thought of them as a unity, as she begins the Long Text: 'This is a revelation of love that Jesus Christ, our endless bliss, made in sixteen showings or revelations particularly.'[19] The scribal introduction to the Short Text reads simply: 'Here is a vision showed by the goodness of God to a devout woman, and her name is

Julian.'[20] A Revelation of Love, then, the various 'showings' being, as it were, facets reflecting different aspects of the one love that is revealed, facets that Julian only gradually came to understand in their full splendour. The extent of the development in her understanding can be seen by comparing the Short Text and the Long Text: whereas the Short Text is an account of her experience, the Long Text is full of long passages of sometimes quite elaborate theological reflection in which she attempts to grapple with the implications of the all-embracing love of God revealed to her, and to us, in the cross of Christ.

One of the longest of these theological reflections in the Long Text – and one that Julian specifically identifies as the fruit of further insight that came to her almost twenty years after the initial visionary experience – is the parable of the lord and the servant, that forms chapter 51 of the Long Text.[21] Julian sees a lord and his servant. The lord sends his servant on an errand, but the servant is so eager to do his lord's will that, as he runs, he falls into a 'slade' – a valley or a boggy marsh – and hurts himself badly. As he lies there hurt, he cannot turn his head to see his lord who is looking at him tenderly and is 'full near'. Julian notes carefully what has happened, and sees that the lord does not at all blame the servant for having fallen down and failed him, 'for only his good will and his great desire was cause of his falling'. Not only that, but Julian hears the lord saying about his servant that not only is he not to be blamed, but that he should be rewarded for all that he has suffered. For Julian this parable is seen to have a double meaning: the servant is both Adam and Christ, his fall is both Adam's fall and Christ's descent into the womb of the Blessed Virgin. Creation and fall – Adam's story – and incarnation and redemption – Christ's story – are held close together, so close that they are the *same story*. The Christian story is not two stories – one ending in disaster, the other the remedying of that disaster – but one story, the story of God's love, that creates, is ever-present, and even incorporates man's sin and rejection of him into its ultimate triumph.

And the story incorporates the imagery of the desert: the desert that, recapitulated in the cell of Julian's vocation, was

71

either the place where her reflection matured, or the place where her reflections finally led her. For the lord is seen, at one stage in her understanding of the parable, as sitting in a desert:

> The place that our lord sat on was simple, on the earth barren and desert, alone in wilderness. His clothing was wide and ample, and full seemly as falleth to a lord; the colour of his cloth was blue as azure, most sad and fair. His expression was merciful, the colour of his face was fair brown with perfect features; his eyes were black, most fair and seemly, full of lovely pity; and within him a high place of refuge, long and broad, all full of endless heavens. And the lovely looking that he looked upon his servant continually, and especially in his falling, methought it might melt our hearts for love and make them burst for joy. The fair looking manifested a seemly mixture which was marvellous to behold: the one was ruth and pity, the other was joy and bliss.[22]

A little later on Julian explains why the lord appeared sitting in a desert:

> But his sitting on the earth barren and desert has this meaning: he made man's soul to be his own city and his dwelling-place, which is most pleasing to him of all his works; and what time that man was fallen into sorrow and pain he was not all seemly to serve of that noble office; and therefore our kind Father would prepare him no other place but to sit upon the earth waiting for mankind, who is mixed with earth, till the time by his grace his dearworthy Son had bought again his city into noble fairness with his hard labour.[23]

The desert has come about because God's true dwelling-place, his city, has been laid waste by man's sin. The idea that the soul is God's kingdom or city is one that had come to Julian in her original visionary experience:

> I saw my soul as large as it were a kingdom; and from the

conditions that I saw therein methought it was a worshipful city. In the midst of this city sits our Lord Jesus Christ, true God and true man, a fair person and of large stature, worshipful, highest Lord.[24]

In the expansion of this in the Long Text, Julian adds that the human soul is God's best and greatest creation: 'he showed the liking that he hath of the making of man's soul; for as well as the Father might make a creature, and as well as the Son could make a creature, so well would the Holy Ghost that man's soul were made; and so it was done'.[25] Because the soul is the greatest and highest of all God's creatures, there is nothing between God and the soul. More precisely – and daringly – Julian says that 'I saw no difference atwix God and our substance',[26] 'our substance' being the inmost, deepest being of our soul or self, which Julian distinguishes from our 'sensuality' – our body and the soul's engagement with the body by means of which the soul communicates with the world and other people. Originally, before sin drove a wedge between our substance and our sensuality, so that we became at odds with ourselves, no longer in touch with ourselves, 'the worshipful city that our Lord Jesus sitteth in . . . is our sensuality in which he is enclosed'.[27] And this state of affairs is restored by the incarnation in which the second person of the Trinity, in uniting himself to our humanity, is united to our sensuality and restores it to unity with our substance.

But what is striking about Julian's understanding of all this is the way in which the 'vertical' relationship between God and the soul is paramount. It was surely her grasp of this that led her into the eremitical life. The fundamental fact about the life of each one of us is the 'vertical', direct, immediate relationship to God. The rupture of that and its restoration in Christ, in his incarnation and passion, is the heart of the Christian story, as Julian sees it. And the rupture of that relationship between God and the soul is best understood as a rupture deep within *ourselves*, the rupture between our substance and our sensuality, our failure to be in touch with what we most deeply are. For, in reality, the rupture between God and the soul is only something that seems to be the case *to us*. If there really were a rupture between God and the soul, the soul would cease to exist: we are held in being by God's love, and God's love is constant; if God were to turn to us in anger we would cease to exist altogether. The 'vertical' relationship between the soul and God is the most fundamental reality there is: it cannot be broken, it can only be obscured. It is the realization of this that lies behind apparently 'selfish' statements such as the saying attributed to Abba Alonius, 'If a man does not say in his heart, in the world there is only myself and God, he will not gain peace', or that famous passage from St Augustine's *Soliloquies*, 'What then do you wish to know? I desire to know God and the soul. Nothing more? Nothing whatever.' It is this realization that lies behind the call to the solitary life. We have already seen that here we touch on a paradox: the solitary is 'separated from all and united to all'. But with Julian we seem to be the other side of the paradox. Her understanding of Christianity is cast in terms of 'God and the soul', but no one could think that Julian was oblivious to other people, who are always present to her in her concern for her 'even-Christians'.

The paramount importance of this vertical relationship means that Julian's interest is focused on God with a kind of absoluteness. This comes out in the two famous images towards the beginning of her Revelation: her seeing the world as a hazelnut, and her seeing God 'in a point'.

> Also in this he showed me a little thing, the quantity of a hazelnut in the palm of my hand; and it was as round as a ball. I looked thereupon with the eye of my understanding and thought: 'What may this be?' And it was generally answered thus: 'It is all that is made.' I marvelled how it might last, for methought that it might suddenly have fallen to nothing for littleness. And I was answered in my understanding: 'It lasteth and ever shall, for God loveth it; and so everything has being by the love of God.'[28]

The first thing that strikes one about this very arresting image is Julian's grasp of the all-embracing nature of God's love that gives being to everything that exists. All that is exists in dependence on God's love, not just on his omnipotent power.

Everything that exists exists because God cares for it. But the 'littleness' – like a hazelnut – of all that is has another meaning for Julian, that is less often noticed:

> It needeth us to have knowing of the littleness of creatures and to nought all thing that is made for to love and have God that is unmade. For this is the cause why we be not all in ease of heart and soul: for we seek here rest in these things that are so little, wherein is no rest, and know not our God that is almighty, all wise, all good; for he is the very rest.[29]

The littleness of all that is does not just speak of the tenderness of God's love for it, it also speaks of its insignificance. Everything that is is tiny, like a hazelnut: the soul should look past it to God who holds it in being. That tiny thing – like a hazelnut – absorbs an enormous amount of our attention, but it is distracting attention from what alone matters: God who created the soul – and everything else – in love, and who can alone satisfy the soul's longing. The vertical relationship between the soul and God is paramount: all else is insignificant in comparison with it. If that vertical relationship – or better that immediate relationship – is forgotten or obscured, then the soul is lost in the maze of finitude and loses its sense of its own worth, even though it can see – as in the picture of the world as a hazelnut – that everything depends on God for its existence:

> But what is to me truly the maker, the keeper, the lover I cannot tell; for, till I am substantially oned to him, I may never have full rest nor true bliss; that is to say, that I be so fastened to him that there is right nought that is made between my God and me.[30]

Another dimension of this emerges when Julian sees 'God in a point'.[31] A 'point' can mean a 'point in time', a moment, or a 'point in space': most commentators prefer the former here. It seems to me, though, that both are intended, and that we perhaps grasp Julian's meaning better if we think of the point spatially. For Julian says that in seeing God in a point, she saw 'that he is in all things'. A point is the smallest interval possible, that which cannot be further subdivided (there is no need to enter into the question as to whether such a notion is rigorously conceivable, whether infinitesimals are possible: that debate began after Julian's day). If God is in a point, in *any* point, then there is no interval – of space or time – where he is not, which is Julian's meaning. As the old medieval definition had it, 'God is a sphere whose centre is everywhere and whose circumference no where': God is everywhere, no where is distant from him (each point is at the centre), and yet nothing circumscribes him (his circumference is nowhere: there is no where beyond him). But if so, Julian wonders, 'what is sin?, for I saw truly that God doth everything be it never so little'. Her conclusion is that 'sin is no deed' – that nothing done is sin, for all that is done is done by God. When she looks to God, and looks at what God shows her, she sees no sin (a vision of hell and purgatory is denied her).[32] But sin is none the less real, and it causes creatures 'great hurt'.[33] Much of the Long Text of the Revelation is given to Julian's wrestling with the seeming contradiction here: a wrestling that reaches its climax in the parable of the lord and the servant. As she seeks to understand this contradiction, she throws up a series of paradoxes, paradoxes in which her conviction of the sole reality of God and his love meets her undeniable experience of the harm done by sin and the reality of her own sin. Among these paradoxes are the most famous of Julian's utterances: 'sin is behovely' – sin is necessary; and 'All shall be well, all manner of thing shall be well'. The conviction that 'all shall be well' is already revealed to her in the Short Text:[34] in the Long Text it becomes a refrain that echoes and re-echoes throughout.[35] 'God in a point' expresses one pole of Julian's conviction: God is everywhere, no where is at all distant from God. But as the parable of the lord and the servant makes graphically clear, that truth is not always experienced as being evident. The fallen servant cannot see that his lord is still very close, and feels the pains of his fallen state (and according to Julian the worst pain is that he cannot see his lord). The other pole of Julian's conviction is that sin lies in the rupture within the soul that obscures God from it, the rupture that tears 'substance' from 'sensuality' and leaves the soul out of contact with itself. Sin is necessary, because the world is fallen, and all of us live in a world that bears the marks of the disruptive effects of sin. But the reality of humanity's broken state is less profoundly true than the reality of God's creative, sustaining love. This must be so, for if God's creative, sustaining love could be nullified there would be nothing to be broken at all: the fact that we are broken and do not disintegrate is due to God's sustaining love. 'All shall be well': because otherwise there would be nothing. But we are still here: it is to that love that keeps us in being that we are to respond.

We are still here: and what it is like to be still here, Julian tried to describe in a long passage that follows on from the parable of the lord and the servant:

All of us that shall be saved, for the time of this life, we have in us a marvellous medley both of weal and woe. We have in us our Lord Jesus arisen; we have in us the wretchedness of the mischief of Adam's falling and dying. By Christ we are steadfastly kept, and by his grace we are raised into sure trust of salvation. And by Adam's falling we are so broken in our feeling in various ways, by sins and by sundry pains, in which we are made dark and so blind that scarcely can we take any comfort. But in our meaning we abide God and faithfully trust to have mercy and grace; and this is his own working in us. And of his goodness he openeth the eye of our understanding by which we have sight, sometimes more and sometimes less, according as God gives ability to take it. And now are we raised into that one, and now are we suffered to fall into that other. And thus is this medley so marvellous in us that we scarcely know of our selves or our even-Christian in what way we stand, for the marvellousness of this sundry feeling; but that each holy assent that we make to God when we feel him, truly willing to be with him with all our heart, with all our soul, and with all our might, then indeed we hate and despise our evil stirrings and all that might be occasion of both spiritual and bodily sin. And yet nevertheless when this sweetness is hidden, we fall again into blindness, and so into woe and tribulation in diverse

77

manners. But then is this our comfort, that we know in our faith that by virtue of Christ, which is our keeper, we never assent thereto, but we strive against it, and endure in pain and woe, praying for that time that he shows him again to us. And thus we stand in this medley all the days of our life.[36]

Our life here is a medley – a mixture – of weal and woe. The medley is reflected in – caused by – the rupture in ourselves between substance – what we are in ourselves – and sensuality – what we are in our engagement with the world. When that rupture is healed, the medley of weal and woe is overcome, 'turning all our blame into endless worship'.[37] And that healing is assured, for our substance – what we are – is grounded in God's love, and still more because in his love God has united our substance and sensuality in the incarnation of his Son. In the medley of weal and woe, the weal is more fundamental. William Blake had much the same vision as Julian in his lines from 'Auguries of Innocence':

> Man was made for Joy and Woe;
> And when this we rightly know
> Thro' the World we safely go,
> Joy and Woe are woven fine,
> A Clothing for the Soul divine;
> Under every grief and pine
> Runs a joy with silken twine.[38]

'Substance', 'sensuality': there is another word that completes Julian's understanding of human nature, and that is 'ground'. Substance is what we are, sensuality is that by which the soul is 'knit to the body' and through the body relates 'horizontally' to other people and to the world. The 'ground' is where we stand, where we derive our being from: it is God himself, for there is nothing between the soul and God, nothing other than God on which the soul can stand.

The notion of the 'ground' of the soul (an idea very important, too, in Eckhart and the Rhineland mystics)[39] is developed by Julian especially in her teaching on prayer. For Julian it is in prayer that we realize the truth of her conviction that 'all shall be well', for in prayer we turn to God in trust and beseech his help and mercy. And we are sure that such prayer is effective, for such prayer rises to God himself *from* God himself. 'I am the ground of thy beseeching,' says Christ to Julian.[40] Prayer, the cry for mercy and help, rises from deep within ourselves. In fact it rises from even more deeply within ourselves than ourselves: prayer rises from the ground of the soul, where our being rests upon the very being of God. In prayer we are caught up in the love of God that is the life of the Trinity:

> Beseeching is a new, gracious, lasting will of the soul oned and fastened into the will of our lord by the sweet, privy work of the Holy Ghost. Our Lord himself, he is the first receiver of our prayers, as to my sight, and taketh it full thankfully and with high enjoyment; and he sendeth it up above and setteth it in treasure where it shall never perish. It is there before God with all his saints, continually received, ever speeding our needs; and when we shall receive our bliss it shall be given us for a degree of joy with endless worshipful thanking of him.[41]

Since prayer is the experiencing of the love and rejoicing of the Holy Trinity, 'prayer oneth the soul to God',[42] and in uniting the soul to God, prayer unites us to the reality in which 'all shall be well'.

'Prayer oneth the soul to God': and God made the human soul in order to dwell in it. Throughout the Revelation Julian uses word-play to drive home the point of her teaching. Here we have an example, for the Middle English verbs meaning to unite and to dwell – to 'one' and to 'wone' – only differ to the ear in the length of the vowel. So in chapter 53 Julian says of the soul that has been made out of nothing by God: 'And thus is the kind (nature) made rightfully oned to the maker, which is substantial kind unmade: that is, God. And therefore it is that there may, nay shall, be right nought between God and man's soul.[43] In the following chapter she goes on to say:

> Highly ought we to rejoice that our soul woneth in God.

Our soul is made to be God's woning place, and the woning place of the soul is God, which is unmade. And high understanding it is inwardly to see and to know that God which is our maker woneth in our soul; and a higher understanding it is inwardly to see and to know our soul, that is made, woneth in God's substance, of which substance, God, we are that we are. And I saw no difference between God and our substance, but as it were all God . . . [44]

The soul is oned to God and woneth in God: is united to God and dwells in him. That is the ultimate truth of what Julian sees. The wonder of that is the source of the joy and cheerfulness that breathes through everything she says. Through *everything* that she says: even as she looks at Christ's dying on the cross, and even as she suffers the pain of sin in this life. As is her way, Julian distinguishes a threefold cheer:

the first is the cheer of the passion as he showed while he was here in this life, dying. Though this beholding be mournful and sorrowful, yet it is glad and merry, for he is God. The second manner of cheer is pity and mercy and compassion: and this he shows to all his lovers with sureness of keeping that belongs to his mercy. The third is the blissful cheer as it shall be without end; and this was oftenest and longest continued. [45]

'Joy and Woe are woven fine . . .' But the joy is only obscured, and what is needed to keep in touch with joy is faith, which is 'none else but a right understanding with true belief and sure trust of our being that we are in God, and God in us, which we see not'. [46]

Julian's desert was a desert that spoke to her in absolutes, a desert that stripped away the conditional, the passing and the transient. In the clear light of the desert she saw God and the soul. But Julian's vision, though absolute, is not austere; or if it is austere in its implications, austerity is not made a virtue in itself. If she sees God and the soul, she sees them as a *city*: God has made the soul to dwell in, to live his life in, and that is the fullest, the most abundant imaginable. We have to go back to the desert to rid ourselves of the clutter of the 'suburbs' that depress and distract, and see the other 'desert', the desert we have made of God's glorious dwelling-place. But the city that Julian sees from her desert, the city in which Julian dwells while in her desert, humanly speaking, is something that is always there, more real than what we take to be reality, only not seen because we no longer look. In faith we are able to discern that 'which we see not', that we are the city in which God dwells. 'Thus I saw and under-stood,' says Julian, 'that our faith is our light in our night; which light is God our endless day.'[47]

NOTES

1 7,000 under Pachomius; 5,000 at Mt Nitria; 10,000 at Arsinoe. Figures listed by Helen Waddell, *The Desert Fathers* (London, 1936), pp. 7 f.

2 See Hans von Campenhausen, 'The ascetic ideal of exile in ancient and early medieval monasticism' in his *Tradition and Life in the Church* (London, 1968), pp. 231–51.

3 See Rotha Mary Clay, *The Hermits and Anchorites of England* (London, 1914).

4 There have been many books and articles on Julian over the last few decades, but there is still no really good book on her. Most recently, see R. Maisonneuve, *L'Univers visionnaire de Julian of Norwich* (Paris, 1987), fascinating but eccentric, with a good bibliography. There are good articles in Marion Glasscoe (ed.), *The Medieval Mystical Tradition in England*, papers given at conferences in Exeter and (later) Dartington (Exeter, 1980 ff). Several good things have appeared from the Sisters of the Love of God in their *Fairacres Publications* (e.g, no. 106, 1988, which includes a valuable piece by Sr Benedicta SLG). The most learned writer on Julian (and the other English mystics) is Dr J. P. H. Clark, whose articles appear mostly in the *Downside Review*. Sheila Upjohn, *In Search of Julian of Norwich* (London, 1989), is a good, brief introduction.

5 The Short and the Long Text are available in a critical edition by E. Colledge OSA and J. Walsh SJ (2 vols, Pontifical Insti-tute of Medieval Studies, Toronto; Studies and Texts, 35; 1978); there is another edition of the Long Text (only) by Marion Glasscoe (Exeter, 1976). For the Long Text, Colledge and Walsh follow the Paris MS, Glasscoe the Sloane MSS in

the British Library. Colledge and Walsh have published a translation of both texts in the *Classics of Western Spirituality* (London, 1978). The best translation of the Long Text is probably the earlier one by J. Walsh (Orchard Classics, 1961); the most accessible translation probably that by Clifton Wolters (Penguin Classics, 1966). The translations in this chapter (deliberately rather literal) are my own.

6 *The Book of Margery Kempe*, bk I, ch. 18 (in the modern version by W. Butler-Bowden, Oxford, The World's Classics, 1954, p. 54).

7 As Sister Benedicta Ward SLG has argued in *Julian Reconsidered* (Fairacres Publications, no. 106, 1988). Though the real value of her argument is less her suggestion that Julian had been married – that remains speculation – than her demonstrating how speculative any definite ideas about Julian's historical circumstances are.

8 E. I. Watkin, *On Julian of Norwich and In Defence of Margery Kempe* (reissued: Exeter, 1979), pp. 3 f. Also the fact that the feast of St John of Beverley falls on 7 May might suggest that the recent celebration of his feast was the reason why he was in Julian's mind: which *might* support the earlier date (that of the Sloane MS) for her showings (though the mention of St John of Beverley only occurs in the later Long Text).

9 Short Text, 6: Colledge-Walsh, p. 220, 11.17 f.

10 David Jones, *Epoch and Artist* (London, 1959), p. 211.

11 For a discussion of the life of a hermit and his relationship to the community rather earlier in medieval England, see H. Mayr-Harting, 'Functions of a 12th-century recluse' in *History*, n.s. 60 (1975), pp. 337–52.

12 I have used James Morton's tr., *The Nun's Rule being the Ancren Riwle* (The Medieval Library, London, 1926).

13 ibid. p. 318.

14 ibid. p. 107.

15 ibid. p. 108.

16 Morton has 'consecrates': I have amended to 'communicates'.

17 ibid. p. 27.

18 See Marion Glasscoe (ed.), *Julian of Norwich: A Revelation of Love* (Exeter, 1976), p. xi.

19 Long Text, 1; Glasscoe, p. 1.

20 Short Text, 1; Colledge-Walsh, p. 201.

21 Glasscoe, pp. 54–61.

22 ibid. pp. 56 f.

23 ibid. p. 57.

24 Short Text, 22; Colledge-Walsh, p. 268.
25 Long Text, 67; Glasscoe, p. 82.
26 Long Text, 54; Glasscoe, p. 65.
27 Long Text, 56; Glasscoe, p. 68.
28 Long Text, 5; Glasscoe, p. 5.
29 ibid.; Glasscoe, pp. 5 f.
30 ibid.; Glasscoe, p. 5.
31 Long Text, 11; Glasscoe, p. 13.
32 Long Text, 33; Glasscoe. pp. 34 f.
33 Long Text, 29; Glasscoe, p. 30.
34 Short Text, 13, 16; Colledge-Walsh, pp. 245, 252.
35 Long Text, 27, 31, 32, 63, 85: Glasscoe, pp. 28 f, 31, 33, 78, 101 (not by any means an exhaustive list).
36 Long Text, 52; Glasscoe, pp. 61 f.
37 Long Text, 52 (last line); Glasscoe, p. 63.
38 *Poetry and Prose of William Blake*, ed. G. Keynes (London, 1927), p. 119; cf. the beginning of the poem 'To see a World in a Grain of Sand / And a Heaven in a Wild Flower' with Julian's parable of the hazelnut.
39 W. Riehle (*The Middle English Mystics*, London, 1981, p. 85) notes an interesting contrast between the English and the German mystics in their use of the word 'ground' (German: *grunt* or *Grund*): whereas for the German mystics it means 'abyss', 'infinite unfathomable depth', for the English mystics it means 'solid ground under our feet', what we stand firmly on.
40 Short Text, 19; Colledge-Walsh, p. 259; Long Text, 41; Glasscoe, p. 42.
41 Long Text, 41; Glasscoe, p. 43.
42 Short Text, 19; Colledge-Walsh, p. 260; Long Text, 43; Glasscoe, p. 45.
43 Glasscoe, p. 64.
44 Long Text, 54; Glasscoe, p. 65.
45 Long Text, 71; Glasscoe, p. 86.
46 Long Text, 54; Glasscoe, p. 65.
47 Long Text, 83; Glasscoe, p. 100.

5

Mount Carmel and St John of the Cross

To associate St John of the Cross with barren mountainous places is quite historical: he was born in 1542 in the village of Fontiveros on the high plateau of Castile and spent many years in the sierras of Andalusia. But it is not, directly, the outer circumstances of St John's life that suggest him as a Desert Father. It is rather the circumstances of his interior life, and his understanding of that life. One of the images he used to express his understanding of that life points us back to the Middle East and the Christian origins of the desert vocation: that is the image of Mount Carmel. It was, of course, not an accident that Mount Carmel was such a powerful image for St John of the Cross. As a young man he had joined the Carmelite order, or to give it its full name, the 'Order of Our Lady of Mount Carmel', and it was the attraction of St Teresa of Avila's attempt to reform the order and restore it to its original vocation as a contemplative, fundamentally eremitical order that kept John in the order.

The order's link with Mount Carmel was quite real, if a matter of past history. Mount Carmel itself lies immediately behind the modern port of Haifa in Israel. It is the place where Elijah the prophet had a contest with the 450 prophets of Baal as to which God was real: Baal could not consume his own sacrifice, but Elijah's God sent down fire to burn up the sacrifice offered to him, even though it had been repeatedly drenched with water. Elijah followed up his religious victory by massacring the unfortunate prophets of Baal (1 Kgs 18). That established a traditional link between Elijah and Mount Carmel, even though it was Mount Horeb, far away in the Sinai desert, where Elijah had his own deepest experience of God. Across the bay of Haifa from Mount Carmel lay the port of Acre which, for most of the thirteenth century, was the capital of the Frankish kingdom established in the Holy Land as a result of the Third Crusade, the kingdom of Outremer.

Exactly how the Carmelite order came to be founded on Mount Carmel is obscure, but by the beginning of the thirteenth century there was a group of hermits who had come from western Europe in the wake of the Crusades living on Mount Carmel, near what was known as St Elijah's cave. They formed a sufficiently cohesive body to feel the need of a simple Rule, which was provided for them in 1209 by Albert, the Latin Patriarch of Jerusalem, under whose jurisdiction they came. According to this Rule, they were to continue a community of hermits, having their meals on their own and praying and saying their office in their cells. They met together each day for the Eucharist, and they were to elect a prior. This state of affairs did not last for long. Within twenty years the Saracens had increased their hold on Mount Carmel. The falling-off in the number of pilgrims, and consequently of their alms, made the hermits' situation more and more precarious. They decided to return to their countries of origin and make new settlements. Around 1242 the English hermits arrived back in England and one of their settlements was at Aylesford in Kent. Their resettlement in the very different (and much colder) countries of western Europe meant that their Rule needed some revision, which took place under the leadership of an Englishman, St Simon Stock (1165–1265), one of the recruits to the order on its return to the West. At the request of the general chapter held at Aylesford in 1247, Pope Innocent IV appointed two Dominicans to deal with the matter and their revised and mitigated form of the Rule, known as the 'Innocentian Rule', was issued later that year. This Rule marks a step from the eremitical to the coenobitic form of life, in that it lays down that the office is to be said in common, rather than individually, and that meals are to be taken in a common refectory, but the life of the Carmelites still remained a completely contemplative and largely solitary life: 'each of you is to stay in his own cell, or near by, pondering the Lord's law day and night and keeping watch at his prayers unless attending to some other duty'.[1]

The Innocentian Rule of 1247 has remained the official text of the Carmelite Rule to the present day: for St Teresa it was the 'primitive' Rule. But the rest of the thirteenth century saw very considerable changes in the Carmelite way of life. They moved with the times, were caught up in the burgeoning life of the cities and were rapidly assimilated to the ethos of the new mendicant orders: the Franciscans and the Dominicans. Like them, they became involved in the new universities and drew many of their novices from the students there. The contemplative life, their inheritance from the desert, suffered. In 1271 Nicolas of Narbonne resigned as Prior General because of the 'utter passing away' of the order's spirit. By 1326 the Carmelite order had been granted full mendicant privileges. The Carmelites were the 'White Friars', and they shared in the mitigations and abuses that characterized the mendicants in the fourteenth century. What had been originally a contemplative, eremitical order became no different from the other mendicant orders, though something of a poor relation. In 1452 an order for women was founded and became very popular. As the sisters were enclosed, their life was closer to the contemplative life that had originally been envisaged than was that of the friars, but nevertheless they shared in the laxer discipline that characterized most religious orders at the end of the Middle Ages.

In the latter half of the sixteenth century, St Teresa sought to reform the Rule and recover its original spirituality of the desert. She had entered the Carmelite convent at Avila in 1535 and lived for twenty years there following the Mitigated Rule, mitigated in such matters as silence and diet. It was only in 1562, after immense difficulty, that she was finally allowed to found her first reformed convent with a few sisters in Avila. They were called 'discalced' Carmelites: one of the 'mitigations' they abandoned was the wearing of shoes. In 1567 she met John of the Cross – than John of St Matthew – and in 1568 he became, with two other friars, one of the first discalced Carmelite friars, at Duruelo, a tiny place between Avila and Salamanca. The carrying through of the reform was no easy matter: the discalced Carmelites were an implicit reproach to the established Carmelite order, which reacted bitterly and forcefully. St John of the Cross himself was imprisoned twice by the friars of the Mitigated Rule: the second time for eight months (December 1577–August 1578) in appalling conditions.

Mount Carmel, as the name and original eremitical inspiration of the order, and thus in a way the beacon of the reform, was a highly charged symbol for John of the Cross. The notion of climbing a mountain was a traditional metaphor for the spiritual life, as we have seen, and this was given particular force in John's conception of the spiritual life as the 'Ascent of Mount Carmel', the title of the first of his great spiritual treatises.

But before we look at what the ascent of Mount Carmel meant for St John, it might be useful to place him not just in the context of the history of his order, but in the context of the history of his times.

Sixteenth-century Spain was a country that had finally escaped from Moorish rule. The Moors – Muslim Arabs – who had invaded the Iberian peninsula in 711, and had at one time ruled the whole of what is now Spain and Portugal apart from the northern province of Asturias, were finally driven out of Spain in 1492. With its final re-establishment as a Christian, a Catholic, country, there came a strong sense of pride in being Spanish and Catholic. This was directed not only against the departing Moors, but also against the sizeable Jewish community that had found *millet* status under the Crescent in Spain preferable to life in the Christian society of the rest of Europe. Jews in Catholic Spain (and earlier in Catholic Castile) were subject to persecution. There were many conversions to Christianity, but even so the taint of Judaism remained with such converts, who were subject to various disabilities (forbidden to hold the rank of *hidalgo* – knight – or to be ordained or join a monastic order, to go to university or join the army) for five generations, according to the letter of the statutes of *limpieza de sangre* (purity of blood). Many converts hid their origin, and the statutes of *limpieza de sangre* were not applied strictly. It appears that one person who would have been hindered by these laws of racial purity was Teresa herself, who was not, as many of her biographers have claimed, of noble Old Christian blood, but the granddaughter of a 'New Christian' ('New' Christians were converts from Judaism) who had lapsed back into Judaism and finally returned to Christianity in Toledo in 1485 under pressure from the Inquisition.[2]

The other side of the proud self-confidence of Catholic Spain in the sixteenth century was a glorious cultural renaissance. Tomás Luis de Victoria, perhaps the greatest religious composer of the Renaissance, was a slightly younger contemporary of St John of the Cross. The poet Góngora was twenty years younger than John, as was the dramatist Lope de Vega. Cervantes, the author of *Don Quixote*, was only five years younger than John. Luís de León, another poet, probably fifteen years his senior, was one of his teachers at the University of Salamanca. The painter El Greco came to Toledo in 1577, the year in which John was imprisoned by the unreformed Carmelites in their priory there. Just to mention these names is to give some idea of the cultural splendour of sixteenth-century Spain, and John of the Cross's own name belongs to that list – as a poet, one of the finest lyric poets of Spain. Indeed if one were to come across John of the Cross for the first time in an anthology of Spanish verse, say the *Penguin Book of Spanish Verse*, one might well wonder what to make of him. The Penguin anthology includes three poems by St John, but only one is ostensibly religious, the last one: 'Verses of the soul that pines to see God'.[3] The other two would be naturally taken to be love poems: one, about a secret meeting under cover of darkness, between a lover and his mistress,[4] the other a passionate poem about the agony and delight of surrender to love.[5] One might think of him as some Jack Donne-John Donne figure: one who wrote passionate love poetry in his youth, and then, after a religious conversion, equally passionate religious poetry.

But the truth is stranger still: those two love poems were, for St John of the Cross himself, religious poems, poems about the encounter between the soul and God in love. The first poem is the basis of two of his treatises on the spiritual life – the *Ascent of Mount Carmel* and the *Dark Night*; and the second is the basis for another such treatise, *The Living Flame of Love*. In fact all his spiritual treatises take the form of a commentary on love poems: his other major treatise, the *Spiritual Canticle*, is a commentary on his poem, 'Songs between the soul and the bridegroom'. That poem, which is a free re-working of the biblical love poem called the Song of Songs, was composed by St John during his eight-month imprisonment in the priory at Toledo. Treatises on the spiritual life in the form of commentaries on love poems must seem rather strange. But the tradition of treating the Song of Songs as a celebration of God's love for the Church, or for the individual soul, was long established among Christians. All John has done, one might say, is to take it *quite seriously*. If a collection of love poems in the Bible is rightly interpreted as about the love between God and the Church (or the soul), then to talk of the spiritual life is to tell a love story, and the soul in love with God (like a young man in love with a girl) will naturally express its love in the form of poems celebrating that love. It is, we readily see, the same John Donne who wrote his teasing, passionate, sometimes querulous, almost bitter love poems and who wrote his 'divine poems', for they are also teasing, passionate, sometimes querulous, even bitter at times. With St John the identity is more complete: poems that can be read as celebrating human love, even human love-making, have a deeper meaning: the love between the soul and God. A *deeper* meaning: because human love is constricted by finitude; its sense of absoluteness, of 'for ever and ever', of a union in which lover and beloved are entirely united, is qualified by the separateness, and by the seemingly final limit of death, that is inherent in the human condition. Human love awakens within the human heart something that can only be fulfilled, can only experience the absoluteness that it senses, *beyond* human love – for Christians, in the soul's loving response to God's love for humankind. '*Oh, noche que juntaste / Amado con Amada, / Amada en el Amado transformada*' ('oh, night that joined Lover with Mistress, the Mistress transformed into the Lover!'): that is what human love yearns for, yet never attains. But between the soul and God, such transformation *is* possible: purified and illuminated by God's love, the soul can be transformed into God, can be 'deified', to use the traditional word that John himself does not hesitate to use.

The story of the soul and God is, then, a love story. So too, as we have seen, was the story of God and Israel in the Old Testament.[6] That story was the story of love that blossomed in the desert (see Hos. 2:14). Similarly, for St John, the love story of the soul and God is expressed in terms of images of negation, privation, like that of the desert. For him, though, the images are the night, darkness, pain, and also the mountain – Mount Carmel. The mountain is a symbol of negation because John is thinking of climbing it, and to climb it one has to strip oneself of unnecessary baggage, make do with few comforts and face much strenuous effort. This experience of negation is central to John's understanding of the night in which the soul's love for God is kindled and nurtured. In John's own life there was one concentrated period of such negation: the eight months during which he was imprisoned by the friars of the Mitigated Rule in their priory in Toledo. As we have already mentioned, it was a period of harsh and cruel punishment for John. He was locked up most of the time in a tiny cupboard-sized room, he was disciplined (that is, flogged) on Fridays and received wounds that never properly healed. He gave way to doubts over whether he was right in his commitment to the reform and wondered whether all this suffering was not punishment for an overweening criticism of his brother friars. Though such doubts caused John of the Cross profound anxiety, they did not break his purpose. Evidence for this is found in his daring, and successful, escape from the priory of Toledo that he carried out in the middle of August 1578. But evidence, too, is found in the poems that he composed during that dark and lonely imprisonment. These poems of his imprisonment certainly included the poems of the *Spiritual Canticle*, a series of eleven poems called *Romances* on the Trinity, creation and incarnation as manifestations of divine love, and a poem with short verses, each ending: '*Aunque es de noche*' ('although it is night'). He may also have composed his poem '*En una noche oscura*' (One dark night') then, but the evidence for that is less firm. The *Romances* explore the heart of John's faith, in the God of love, a Trinity of persons bound together in love, whose love is manifest in creation and the incarnation. In the other poems there are persistent images of night and darkness, but a night and darkness that set off the power of faith:

> This living fount which is to me so dear
> Within the bread of life I see it clear
> Though it be night.[7]

Or a night about to pass into the glories of the new day:

> Before the dawn comes round
> Here is the night, dead-hushed with all its glamours,
> The music without sound,
> The solitude that clamours,
> The supper that revives us and enamours.[8]

Whether or not St John wrote the poem 'One dark night' in prison at Toledo, it is this poem, and the two treatises based on it – the *Ascent of Mount Carmel* and the *Dark Night* – that explore most thoroughly the imagery of negation, especially that of night and darkness. As a preface to these two works (which we shall treat as a single whole)[9] there is a kind of sketch map of Mount Carmel. In later editions of the *Ascent* this map came to take the form of a more or less elaborate engraving,[10] but John's original version is very simple and basic.[11] At the top is the summit of Mount Carmel. 'Only the honour and glory of God dwell on this mount' is written at the centre; this motto is surrounded by the names of virtues – peace, joy, happiness, delight, wisdom, justice, fortitude, charity, piety; on each side are inscribed further mottoes – 'glory matters nothing to me', 'suffering matters nothing to me' (there are various other mottoes too). Three paths lead on to the Mount: to the right and to the left are the 'ways of imperfect spirit'; in the centre is 'the path of Mount Carmel, the perfect spirit'. The ways of imperfect spirit lead up the mountain, but stop short of the summit (the later engravings have them wandering off into the foothills): one is labelled 'goods of heaven: glory, joy, knowledge, consolation, rest', and the other 'goods of earth: possessions, joy, knowledge, consolation, rest'. St John seems to make no real distinction between these two ways of 'imperfect spirit' (the engravings sometimes make the way of the 'goods of heaven' a circuitous route to the summit, while the way of the 'goods of earth' wanders off altogether – but such a moralizing

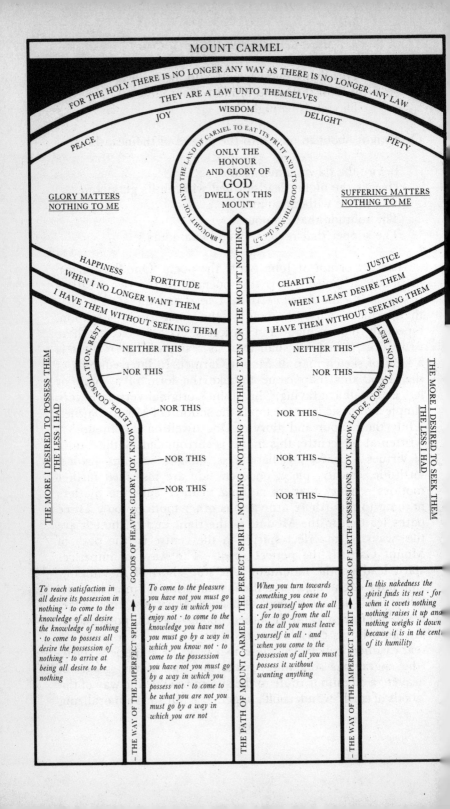

interpretation is far from John's intention).[12] At the top of
each of these two ways is a motto: 'The more I desired to
possess (or seek) them, the less I had.' The way up the
middle, the path of Mount Carmel, of perfect spirit, is: *'nada,
nada, nada, nada, nada, nada, y aun en el Monte nada'* ('nothing . . .
and even on the Mount nothing'). It is clearly marked off
from the ways of imperfect spirit: against each of the 'goods'
is a mark: 'nor this'. The way of perfection is presented as a
way of unremitting negation. Along the bottom of the sketch
of Mount Carmel are four verses:

To reach satisfaction in all
desire its possession in nothing
To come to the knowledge of all
desire the knowledge of nothing
To come to possess all
desire the possession of nothing
To arrive at being all
desire to be nothing

To come to the pleasure you have not
you must go by a way in which you enjoy not
To come to the knowledge you have not
you must go by a way in which you know not
To come to a possession you have not
you must go by a way in which you possess not
To come to be what you are not
you must go by a way in which you are not

When you turn towards something
you cease to cast yourself upon the all
For to go from the all to the all
you must leave yourself in all
And when you come to the possession of all
you must possess it without wanting anything

In this nakedness the spirit
finds its rest, for when it
covets nothing, nothing
raises it up, and nothing

weighs it down, because it is
in the centre of its humility.[13]

These verses (which have something about them of the feel
of the sayings of the ancient Greek philosopher Heraclitus,
the 'Riddler' or the 'Obscure' – or the 'Dark', *skoteinos*) are
certainly uncompromising, and underline the *nada, nada, nada*
of the way of perfect spirit. But like Heraclitus, these verses
have a kind of riddling obviousness: especially the second set.
If you really want to get to somewhere where you are not,
you must move from where you are and travel through where
you are not. If you are unwilling to abandon the familiar
place where you are, then you will never arrive anywhere.
Abraham's faith was manifested in his going out from his
'country and kindred and his father's house' (Gen. 12:1). The
third set of verses makes clear the radicalism of the first set.
To choose something, some *particular* thing, is to turn away
from everything, from the all. If then you set your sights on
the all, you must turn away from everything, from any particular thing. Nothing is the way to the all; for anything will
block your receptiveness to the all.

The Night, Darkness, the steep ascent of Mount Carmel:
these are not for St John of the Cross ends in themselves,
they are images for the way that leads from what the women
in T. S. Eliot's *Murder in the Cathedral* call 'living, and partly
living' to what John calls 'possession of all', 'being all'. In this
St John is not far from the very different-sounding teaching of
Thomas Traherne, that 'you must want like a GOD, that you
may be satisfied like GOD'[14] and that 'wants are Bands and
Cements between God and us'.[15] For both of them – the
sixteenth-century Spanish Carmelite and the seventeenth-
century Anglican priest – we are beings who want and desire:
only too often our wants and desires are exhausted without
being satisfied, because they are directed not towards God,
but towards possession of one or other (or even many) of his
creatures. If our desire, our longing, is to be truly fulfilled,
really satisfied, then we must learn to want what can fulfil
our longing, we must learn to want (or that we want) the all
as infinite, rather than the all as totality (which we can

disguise as merely many, or even just something): and that longing will entail a good deal of unlearning.

It is this *un*learning that the Night invites us to, that it imposes upon us. St John of the Cross explains, in several places, what he means by his imagery of the Night. At the beginning of the *Ascent* he says that 'night' means purgation or purification: these periods of purification are called nights because in them 'the soul journeys in darkness as though by night' (I.1.1).[16] He then distinguishes between various nights in a number of ways. He distinguishes between a night of the sensory part of the human being, and a night of its spiritual part; he also distinguishes between active purgation and passive purgation (I.1.2). The first night is 'the lot of beginners, at the time God commences to introduce them into the state of contemplation'; the second night takes place 'in those who are already proficients, at the time God desires to lead them into the state of divine union. This purgation, of course, is more obscure, dark, and dreadful . . .' (I.1.3). In all this there are really two dichotomies at work: that between sense and spirit, and that between active and passive. The distinction between sense and spirit reflects the medieval understanding of the human person. The human person engages with the outside world, of things and people, through the senses: sight, hearing, touch, smell, taste. Everything we know about the world around us we learn through the senses: a 'night of the senses', then, denies us all that, so that the soul becomes empty, dark. 'Spirit' refers to the human person in his or her inwardness, the spiritual faculties of memory, understanding and will: the purification of these is more radical, more difficult and more painful – more like pulling up a plant by the roots than simply pruning it. The dichotomy between active and passive is rather different. This refers to the quality of human engagement in the purifying night. The active night is the purification in which we participate, by self-denial, by trust in God, by our own attempts to purify ourselves of all that distances us from God. The passive night is the purification to which we submit – passively – by letting God work in us, purifying us by his own cleansing touch. Both dichotomies are progressive: the night begins with the senses and progresses to the spirit, it begins as active and later becomes

passive. The onset of the night is a relatively common experience, but few persevere into the deeper reaches of the night.

At the beginning of chapter 2 of Book I of the *Ascent*,
John of the Cross offers three reasons for calling this 'journey
towards union with God' a night:

> the first has to do with the point of departure, because the
> individual must deprive himself of his appetite for worldly
> possessions. This denial and privation is like a night for all
> his senses. The second reason refers to the means or road
> along which a person travels to this union. Now this road
> is faith, and for the intellect faith is also like a dark night.
> The third reason pertains to the point of arrival, namely,
> God. And God is also a dark night to man in this life.
> These three nights pass through a soul, or better, the soul
> passes through them in order to reach divine union with
> God. (I.2.1)

A few paragraphs further on, John emphasizes that:

> in actuality these three nights comprise only one night, a
> night divided into three parts, just as the natural night.
> The first part, the night of the senses, resembles early
> evening, that time of twilight when things begin to fade
> from sight. The second part, faith, is completely dark, like
> midnight. The third part, representing God, is like the
> early dawn just before the break of day. (I.2.5)

For St John, as we have already seen, the human being is a
being of *desires*: at the heart of our being is a deep longing, a
love that aches to be satisfied. This longing seeks satisfaction
in the world in which we live: possessions, experiences of one
kind or another (sometimes 'ecstatic' experiences: religious
exaltation, sex, overwhelming beauty – in art, music, and so
on), power, whether through wealth or knowledge. All these
beckon to us, awaken our desire and promise fulfilment. But
that promise is vain: they may exhaust, but they cannot fulfil.
The night is a night in which these desires are cut off, or
rather banked up for divine union, which will fulfil and is the
goal of the night. John is quite radical about the cutting-off

of desire: half-measures will leave us lurking in the twilight. But the journey is only possible if there has been awakened in the soul a longing for God that already senses the vanity of human desire: if the heart has woken up 'with the drawing of this love and the voice of this calling', to quote from *The Cloud of Unknowing*[17] (which John may possibly have known). The 'passive' element is always there: no one enters the night, not even the active night, under one's own steam, one is drawn there by responding to God's call. But the night is a *night*: it deprives us of any capacity to fend for ourselves – 'faith' and 'trust' (both of which can, significantly, be 'blind') are what is called for. Denial of the senses, the way of faith, the ultimate and overwhelming reality of God: this is what St John says the night is about.

In his treatise, the *Dark Night*, which is a sequel to the *Ascent of Mount Carmel*,[18] St John returns to explaining his imagery of the night. At *Dark Night* I.8.1 he identifies the night with contemplation, and goes on to say that the night of the senses is common, but that few persevere into the night of the spirit, that the first purgation is 'bitter and terrible to the senses', but is nothing compared to the second purgation, which is 'horrible and frightful to the spirit'. Most of this repeats what we have already learnt from the *Ascent*, but the identification of the night and contemplation strikes a somewhat different note. When John speaks of contemplation, he is taking for granted a distinction that had become traditional in the West by the end of the Middle Ages (though it has not in fact very deep roots in the Christian tradition):[19] the distinction between meditation and contemplation. According to this distinction, meditation is a form of prayer that makes active use of the reason and imagination: in my prayer I imagine (say) a scene from the gospels and try to enter into it, see what it means for me, try to respond with love, repentance and commitment. It is a form of prayer that depends on images: these images inspire my feelings and devotion. Contemplation, on the other hand, dispenses with images, the reason and the imagination are ignored or suppressed, and prayer becomes a kind of alert attentiveness in the darkness where God is. Contemplation is understood to be a higher form of prayer than meditation: meditation prepares the soul for contemplation. For St John contemplation is the prayer of the night: it is watching in darkness, freed from the distractions of thoughts and images. Twice – in *Ascent* II.13 and *Dark Night* I.9 – John lists three signs by which the soul may know that it should pass from meditation to contemplation. These are: (1) the soul can find satisfaction in nothing, neither God nor creatures; (2) the soul still longs for God and is troubled that it can no longer pray in the way it was accustomed to (meditation) and thinks that it is turning away from God and deserting him; (3) the soul *cannot* meditate or make use of discursive reason or the imagination in prayer – when it tries to do so, it feels distracted and drawn away from God (very similar teaching about the onset of contemplation is to be found in the last chapter of *The Cloud of Unknowing*). These signs demonstrate that the soul is genuinely being drawn by God to the prayer of contemplation, and not simply upset or depressed (when the soul's longing for God – see (2) – would be lost along with everything else). They are really tests that the soul has no choice: for John the only sure sign that the soul is being called, and not just fancying itself as an advanced pray-er. We are drawn into the darkness – 'with the drawing of this love and the voice of this calling' – we do not venture into it out of curiosity, or a sense of adventure.

St John frequently comes back to this teaching about the beginning of contemplation. It is treated in both the *Ascent* and the *Dark Night*, as we have seen, and he comes back to it again in the long digression on spiritual directors (and their failings) in the *Living Flame* (III.30–62), though there his immediate point is the damage directors can do to souls on the brink of divine union. But the point seems to be that the transition to contemplation, though not an 'advanced' stage, is a crucial stage in the individual's life of prayer. Here it learns to 'let go', to let God pray in the soul, as it were: and this 'letting go', this surrender into God's hands, is the crucial lesson to learn if we are to live in the night and submit to God's purifying touch. One of the most distressing things about contemplation, St John says, is the sense one has that it is a waste of time, that one is doing nothing, because one can *do* nothing. John explains the nature of this apparently 'useless' passivity by means of a metaphor:

> For if such a soul should desire to make any effort of its own with its interior faculties, this means that it will hinder and lose the blessings which, by means of that peace and ease of the soul, God is instilling into it and impressing upon it. It is just as if some painter were painting or dyeing a face; if the sitter were to move because he desired to do something, he would prevent the painter from accomplishing anything and would disturb him in what he was doing. And thus, when the soul desires to remain in inward ease and peace, any operation and affection and attention wherein it may then seek to indulge will distract it and disquiet it and make it conscious of aridity and emptiness of sense.[20]

In yet another place, St John returns to the question of the meaning of the imagery of the night. In Book II of the *Dark Night*, he begins once again his exposition of the poem, *'En una noche oscura'*, and comments: 'this dark night is an inflowing of God into the soul' (II.5.1). But this, he says, raises a question: 'Why is the Divine Light . . . here called by the soul a dark night?' (II.5.2). He gives two reasons why 'this Divine Wisdom is not only night and darkness for the soul, but is likewise affliction and torment'. 'The first is because of the height of Divine Wisdom, which transcends the talent of the soul, and in this way is darkness to it; the second, because of its vileness and impurity, in which respect it is painful and afflictive to it, and is also dark.'

The first reason is the 'height of Divine Wisdom'. God's light appears to us as darkness because it is dazzling, overwhelming. St John is here drawing on that tradition of theology (Greek in origin) that lays emphasis on God's unknowability: it is the radical unknowability of God that makes his light seem dark to us. John, in fact, refers to Denys the Areopagite for support here. As we come close to God, and begin to catch a glimpse of his own reality, rather than reflections of his power in the created order, we are overwhelmed by his unknowability, we are filled with awe and wonder. And this is a kind of darkness: it is not a light that

throws light on our plans and desires, it is a light that out-
shines everything and leaves us overwhelmed.

St John's second reason as to why God's light appears dark
turns on our own radical sinfulness and impurity: it is dark
because it shows up the darkness in our being, and in showing
it up begins to purify it. But that process of purification is
something we resist, we are attached to the 'selves' we have
fashioned out of our attachment to creaturely things; a radical
purity seems to open up on to something entirely unknown.

This meeting in the dark night of contemplation between
God's light and our darkness is what is involved in passive
purifying.

> The Divine assails the soul in order to renew it and thus
> make it divine; and, stripping it of the habitual affections
> and attachments of the old man, to which it is very closely
> united, knit together and conformed, destroys and con-
> sumes its spiritual substance, and absorbs it in deep and
> profound darkness. (II.6.1)

For the soul this is experienced as a 'perishing and melting
away', a 'cruel spiritual death': it feels like Jonah swallowed
by the great fish, 'for in this sepulchre of dark death it must
needs abide until the spiritual resurrection which it hopes
for'. The soul feels that God has abandoned it, that it is
deserted and misunderstood by all, especially its friends. In
the next few chapters John goes on to give an account of
this experience of torment and dereliction, and illustrates his
account by quotations from Scripture: the reference to Jonah
already noticed, quotations from the Psalms and from the
experience of the prophet Jeremiah. A point that we may
miss, but John's original readership would not have missed,
is that these examples from the Old Testament were understood as foreshadowing Christ, his agony and his passion. For
St John the dark night is the way of the cross, it is living out
that death into which we were baptized that we may make
our own the experience of resurrection. These chapters (5–8)
were described by Allison Peers as 'brilliant beyond all
description; in them we seem to reach the culminating point
of their author's mystical experience'.[21]

As we have said, the dark night is not, for St John, an end: it is a way, or as he puts it himself, a journey. But so too is this life: a journey through the night towards the kingdom. For John the spiritual life is being called into the night, up the mountainside, into the desert: the most immediate choice for us is whether we respond or whether we shrink from what that response entails. St John speaks of the night in terms of uncompromising negativity: not for nothing does he see the way of perfect spirit as *'nada, nada, nada'*. But as the verses at the bottom of his sketch of Mount Carmel suggest, this radical negation is the price of gaining all. Not for a moment does John deny the fundamental goodness of all that God has created: it is simply that the creature can absorb our attention and block out God. The purified soul is given back, as it were, the whole created order and can now delight in it without striving to possess it. That is seen most clearly in his *Spiritual Canticle*, where John's love for created beauty finds expression:

> The breathing air so keen;
> The song of Philomel: the waving charm
> Of groves in beauty seen:
> The evening so serene,
> With fire that can consume yet do no harm.[22]

On this verse John comments:

> The soul also greatly desires to see the beauty of the grove; this is the grace and wisdom and beauty which not only does each of the creatures have from God, but which they cause among themselves in their wise and ordered mutual correspondence, both of the higher creatures and of the lower; this is to know the creatures by the contemplative way, which is a thing of great delight, for it is to have knowledge concerning God.[23]

The night is, finally and fundamentally, a night of love. As the night purifies the soul, so it comes to know and perceive its Beloved. Here again creation that has been denied is given back to it. As John of the Cross seeks to celebrate the love

101

between the soul and God, he follows the Song of Songs in drawing on the idea of creation, in all its splendour, as speaking to the soul of the wonder and greatness of God's love:

> My Love's the Mountain range,
> The valleys each with solitary grove,
> The islands far and strange,
> The streams with sounds that change,
> The whistling of the lovesick winds that rove.[24]

NOTES

The most up-to-date critical edition of the Spanish text of St John of the Cross is the eleventh edition published in the *Biblioteca de Autores Cristianos* (vol. 15, Madrid, 1982), prepared by Luciano Ruano de la Iglesia OCD. I have used two English translations for the prose works: that by E. Allison Peers (3 vols, new edn, London, 1953) and that by Kieran Kavanaugh OCD and Otilio Rodriguez OCD (Edinburgh, 1966). Of these two translations, Allison Peers' is meticulously accurate, but suffers from his attempt to 'reproduce the atmosphere of a sixteenth-century text as far as is consistent with clarity' (op. cit. vol. 1, p. xviii); the translation by Frs Kavanaugh and Rodriguez is freer, but more readable. For the poems of St John, I have used the fine translation by Roy Campbell (London, 1951). The bibliography on St John of the Cross is enormous, and most of it in Spanish: Fr Luciano Ruano provides an extensive bibliography in his edition (ed. cit. pp. 925–41). Both Allison Peers and Kieran Kavanaugh provide valuable introductory material in their translations. The standard work in English on the Carmelites (both Teresa and John) is E. W. Trueman Dicken, *The Crucible of Love* (London, 1963). For St John's life, see the biographies by Crisógono de Jesús (Eng. tr., London, 1958) and by Gerald Brenan (Cambridge, 1973). See also Ruth Burrows, *Ascent to Love* (London, 1987), Alain Cugno, *St John of the Cross* (Eng. tr, London, 1982), and H. U. von Balthasar, *The Glory of the Lord*, vol. 3 (Eng. tr., Edinburgh, 1986), pp. 105–71.

1   This account of the early history of the Carmelite order is taken from a paper given by the late Sister Jocelyn Mary SLG, from whom I have learnt much about Carmel and St John. I

have made use of the paper with the permission of the Reverend Mother Superior SLG.

2 See Gerald Brenan, op. cit. Appendix I, 'St Teresa's Jewish ancestry', pp. 91–5.
3 *The Penguin Book of Spanish Verse*, ed. J. M. Cohen (Harmondsworth, 1956), pp. 182–5.
4 ibid. pp. 179–81.
5 ibid. pp. 181 f.
6 See, in addition to the passages cited above, pp. 32 f, Hos. 11:8; Ezek. 16.
7 Roy Campbell's tr. p. 47.
8 ibid. p. 19.
9 It is generally accepted nowadays that, although the text of the *Ascent of Mount Carmel* is incomplete, the *Dark Night* forms a kind of conclusion to that work: see Trueman Dicken, pp. 216–22 and K. Kavanaugh's introd. to his and O. Rodriguez's tr., pp. 54 f.
10 See plates III, V, and VI in Trueman Dicken, op. cit.
11 See plates IV (the original) and VII (English version) in ibid.; also Kavanaugh-Rodriguez, pp. 66 f. And see the diagram on p. 92, based on the frontispiece to Ruth Burrows, *Ascent to Love* (Darton, Longman and Todd, 1987).
12 On the way in which the engravings misinterpret and embroider St John's teaching, see Trueman Dicken, pp. 237–44.
13 Kavanaugh-Rodriguez's tr., p. 67.
14 *Centuries of Meditation* I.44, in Thomas Traherne, *Centuries, Poems and Thanksgivings*, ed. H. M. Margoliouth, vol. I (Oxford, 1958), p. 22.
15 *Centuries* I.51 (ed. cit. I, p. 25).
16 Translation used is that by Kavanaugh and Rodriguez.
17 *The Cloud of Unknowing* 2.
18 See note 9 above.
19 See Simon Tugwell, *Ways of Imperfection* (London, 1984), chs 10 and 11, pp. 103–24.
20 *Dark Night* I. 10.5; Allison Peers' tr., vol. 1, p. 358.
21 Allison Peers, vol. 1, p. 318.
22 Campbell's tr., p. 27.
23 *Spiritual Canticle* (First Redaction), 38.8; Allison Peers' tr., vol. 2, p. 171.
24 Campbell, p. 19.

6

The Devils of Loudun and Père Surin

The demonic possession of the Ursuline nuns at Loudun, in
Poitou south of the river Loire, in the 1630s – the theatrical
exorcisms, the terrible fate of the parish priest Urbain Grandier, who was burnt to death as a 'magician' – are better
known in England than might be expected. This fame is
probably almost entirely due to Aldous Huxley's rather
superior treatment of the events in his work, *The Devils of
Loudun*, and, based on that, Ken Russell's somewhat sen-
sational film of the same title. Even though better-known than
might be expected, these events must seem very remote from
the theme of the desert. However, one of the people caught
up in these events was a young Jesuit priest, Père Jean-Joseph
Surin, one of the exorcists at Loudun, to whose care the
prioress of the Ursulines, Jeanne des Anges, was entrusted.
As Huxley reveals in the final chapter of his book, Surin's
involvement in the events of Loudun was at very great personal cost: for years afterwards he was profoundly disoriented
in his mind, for a time unable to speak, several times driven
to attempt suicide, and for twenty years unable to look after
himself. For Surin, the events of Loudun led him into a desert
of the mind: the desolation of insanity.

At the very beginning of this book we suggested that the
image of the desert could be understood in various ways: both
externally and inwardly, both as an ideal that attracts as a
place of spiritual experience, and as a place of desolation that
is not at all sought out but rather imposed. So far we have
explored both the external and the interior desert, but for the
most part we have seen the desert as a place of spiritual
experience, a place where God is to be found, that is sought

out . . . in various ways. Surin presents us with the desert as a place that no one would seek, but to which some find themselves condemned: an interior desert, a place of desolation. The contrast between choice and imposition cannot, however, be drawn too sharply. Surin himself points out that in St Mark's account of the temptation of Christ, Jesus is *driven* into the desert by the Spirit: the desert is less chosen by Christ than imposed on him, but is nevertheless seen as a place of profound spiritual experience:

> I imagine that our Lord's going into the desert was an utter absorption in the greatness of his Father and a profound recourse to this marvellous abyss of truths, of riches and of divine delights, in which the holy soul of Jesus Christ advanced by the impulsion of the divine Spirit who led him and, as the Gospel says, thrust him strongly into the desert. That is an example for us, to follow him into this very abyss of God, drawing us more into this divine desert which is the vast solitude of God, which is not barren like earthly deserts that are only sand.[1]

Despite this blurring between choice and imposition, Surin's own experience of the desert, an inner desert of madness, is not something that anyone would, or even perhaps could, seek out for themselves. To understand Surin's experience of the desert, it is necessary to set it in the context of his life. His madness was a consequence of his involvement, as an exorcist, in the events of Loudun: so to understand it we shall have to look, necessarily briefly, at these events. But Surin's madness was a kind of interlude in his life: after some twenty years he emerged from his madness and began a demanding and remarkable ministry as spiritual director and preacher. His spiritual direction was conducted mainly through his letters – 446 of which have survived from the period from 1657 – some of which constitute veritable treatises on the spiritual life. In addition there are the various parts of his *Catéchisme spirituel* (especially the last part, called the *Guide spirituel*, which was only published in this century), not to mention his *Cantiques spirituels* and *Poésies spirituelles*. As a preacher, he preached in the convents of Bordeaux (where he lived most of his life) and latterly in the villages in the surrounding countryside. The quite remarkable quality of insight and understanding manifest in this final period of his life led Henri Bremond to herald Surin as 'a master . . . who has, for us, the same importance in the spiritual order as Boileau in the literary order':[2] such spiritual mastery was the fruit of his struggles in the desert of his madness, just as the Desert Fathers had won theirs in their ascetic struggles in the Egyptian desert.

Our method, then, will be to sketch the life of Père Surin, drawing attention particularly to all that bears on his experience of the desert of insanity, and then to look at his spiritual teaching, again concentrating on what seems to bear the signs of his desert experience.

Jean-Joseph Surin was born in 1600 into a wealthy and well-connected Bordeaux family. The Surins (or Seurins) were Catholic, pious and generous – especially, it seems, to the Jesuits and Carmelites in Bordeaux – which may explain, as Bremond observes, 'the strange liberty that was extended to Père Surin during the years of his sickness'.[3] Surin had a very happy childhood: in later years he looked back especially to a wonderful autumn he spent in the countryside near to Bordeaux when he was eight. Because of an outbreak of the plague in the city, he was sent:

> to a house in the country, close to the city, in a very beautiful spot, in the most lovely season of the year, and left alone with a governess whose sole concern was to make me happy; and each day I was visited by my relatives who, one after another, came to see me and brought me presents. The whole day was given to playing and going for walks, without fear of anyone. After this few weeks, I was sent to school and my bad times began.[4]

This reminiscence comes from one of his many letters to Jeanne des Anges. In another letter, this time to the prioress of the Carmel at Toulouse, he speaks of his acquaintance with Mother Isabelle des Anges, one of the disciples of St Teresa of Avila, who had come to France at the invitation of Cardinal de Bérulle to establish a Carmelite convent of the

Reform in Bordeaux. In that letter[5] he calls her his 'spiritual mother'; elsewhere he says that 'on holidays I sometimes went to see Mother Isabelle des Anges, a Spaniard, who was the Mother Prioress and who had created the foundation'.[6] This early link with the reformed Carmelites is important, as Surin was deeply influenced by the writings of St John of the Cross and St Teresa of Jesus, and some of his later reflection on the desert is developed for the sake of the Carmel at Bordeaux to which he wrote regularly: the series of letters to them are particularly important for his later teaching.

When he was sixteen Surin became a Jesuit novice and began his training. He did his philosophy at the famous college of La Flèche from 1619 to 1623, and then went to Paris, to the Collège de Clermont, for his theology. In 1625 he came back to Bordeaux, where he completed his theological studies and was ordained priest in 1626. In 1629 he did his 'third year' at Rouen, where Père Lallemant was teaching: that 'third year' under Père Lallemant was profoundly important for Surin who was very receptive to his teaching.[7] Surin then began his ministry as a Jesuit priest, first at Bordeaux, then at Saintes, and in 1632 he went to Marennes. It was in 1632 that the possession of the nuns at Loudun began, but it was only at the end of 1634 that Surin himself was sent there as an exorcist; by then the parish priest, Urbain Grandier, who had incurred Cardinal Richelieu's enmity, had been tortured and burnt at the stake, accused by the possessed nuns themselves of having caused their demonic possession. Bremond quotes the testimony of one of the Jesuits involved: 'Grandier was condemned on the constant and uniform witness of the Father of lies!'[8] The events of Loudun, however, involved more than the personal trajectories of those involved, however frightful or however bizarre. Michel de Certeau, Surin's modern editor, remarks:

> their poor personal adventures were swallowed up in a much greater drama: the holy war between the Huguenots and the Catholics, the political struggle between the feudalism of the provinces and the power of the king, the crisis that rocked the economic equilibrium, the social hierarchy and the very foundations of contemporary attitudes.[9]

In particular, the exorcisms themselves were public theatrical displays: the exorcists used the wretched minds and bodies of the nuns as a kind of arena in which a supposed supernatural combat was played out. The power of the exorcists to cure possession (after a tasteless demonstration of the presence of demons) was not displayed for the sake of the possessed, but was a powerful piece of Catholic weaponry in the struggle between Catholic and Protestant. Protestants were taunted by Catholics with their failure to achieve miraculous cures, and the Catholic miracles converted many a Protestant to Catholicism. As Keith Thomas has remarked, speaking primarily of the English scene:

> It was no wonder that the recusant clergy attracted crowds of admirers when they began their well-publicized campaign of dispossession in 1586. 'In the compass of half a year,' estimated a contemporary, no 'fewer . . . were by that means reconciled to the Church of Rome than five hundred persons: some have said three or four thousand.' Fresh tales of exorcism were brought back by Continental travellers: it was after witnessing the exorcism of the Ursuline nuns at Loudun in 1635 that the courtier and diplomat Walter Montagu was converted to Popery.[10]

When Surin arrived at Loudun in December 1634 as an exorcist, he was assigned the prioress, Jeanne des Anges, whose 'confessions' had been the principal evidence against Grandier (though on his death she had quickly begun to accuse herself of perjury and at one point had tried to commit suicide). Jeanne des Anges is a rather unattractive personality. Bremond quickly loses patience with her and her exhibitionism: 'if Jeanne des Anges had been, I do not say a saint, but simply a good religious, it would appear most likely that the trial of Urbain Grandier would never have taken place'.[11] Michel de Certeau presents a much more nuanced account of her.[12] For us she is important as the one with whom Surin had to deal, at Loudun and thereafter. As an exorcist, he treated her very differently from the way she had been treated so far. He replaced the public exorcisms with what amounted to spiritual direction – of her as a woman and a nun. Instead

108

of making her perform (something she was, perhaps, only too eager to do), he taught her to pray. Instead of treating her as 'thing possessed', he treated her as a daughter of God, he spoke to her quietly about God her Father, he tried to bring her into a free relationship with her Creator and Redeemer. Not that Surin underestimated the seriousness of her demonic possession: it would be a great mistake to imagine that Surin treated Jeanne as suffering from a psychological disorder rather than demonic possession, for all that his treatment of her seems like a form of psychotherapy that has been heralded as constituting 'such an important progress that it bears the mark of genius'.[13] Indeed it is only by taking Jeanne des Anges' affliction at least as seriously as Surin did (whether we express it in the same terms or not), that we can understand its significance for Surin himself. In one of his accounts of the events of Loudun (which he regarded for the rest of his life as a signal victory over the powers of evil), Surin says:

> One day, as I prayed, I could not stop myself from offering myself to the divine Majesty to take on myself the evil of this religious [Jeanne des Anges] and to experience all her sensations, to the point of being possessed by the devil, so long as it pleased the divine Goodness to give her the grace to enter solidly into the practice of virtue, myself wishing for nothing with such passion as to deliver this soul from the captivity of the devil.[14]

Thus Surin embarked on what, in a different context, Charles Williams has called the 'way of Substitution and Exchange',[15] but with a rare literalism. As the exorcisms progressed, Surin himself came to experience a growing invasion of the power of evil. On 10 May 1635, after a session of exorcism, he had what sounds like a heart attack, which was followed by a long period of depression.[16] On 3 May 1636, the feast of the Invention of the Cross, he had a premonition that he would experience great evils for twenty years, and the thought of twenty years filled him with fear.[17] Another year was to pass before the final exorcism of Jeanne des Anges, some months of which (October 1636-June 1637) were spent back in Bordeaux, where he had been recalled partly because of anxieties

109

about his health, and partly because of doubts by his superiors about his approach to exorcism. The final exorcism of Jeanne took place in October 1637. Two things about it are striking, and highlight the two sides of Surin's exorcism of the Ursuline nun. The first is that this final 'exorcism' took the form of a retreat, based on the *Spiritual Exercises* of St Ignatius Loyola. In other words the final 'exorcism' was conceived of as a decisive step in Jeanne des Anges' spiritual formation. The second point seems to belong to another world: the last demon, who called himself Behemoth, only agreed to come out of Jeanne, if she and Père Surin made a pilgrimage to the tomb of St Francis de Sales at Annecy, in Savoy: the demon departed when Jeanne made a vow to make such a pilgrimage. They made their journey together from April to September 1638, but by that time Surin himself had embarked on another journey, an inner journey, into the desolation of madness.

For Jeanne des Anges, however, the pilgrimage to Annecy was one of the high points of her life, a kind of triumphal procession during which they visited Tours, Paris, Moulins, Nevers, Lyon, Grenoble and Annecy itself. Everywhere she was the centre of attention, a kind of living relic, with her hand bearing the names, superimposed one on another, of Jesus, Mary, Joseph and Francis de Sales, that had been inscribed by the demons who had possessed her, and her chemise stained with the ointment of St Joseph, again the product of one of the sessions of exorcism. A living miracle, she received the veneration of Members of Parliament, gentlemen of high society, bishops, members of the Condé family, Cardinal Richelieu, Queen Anne of Austria and Louis XIII himself.[18]

On his return Surin went to live in the college at Bordeaux, where he was to spend the rest of his life. He sank quickly into a state of total prostration. Surin himself later dated this from the winter of 1637–8, but it is hard to imagine that he accomplished the pilgrimage to Annecy as a bedridden invalid, so perhaps during those months he had a period of respite. In 1660 he described his experience in these terms (referring to himself in the third person):

He found himself practically incapable of doing anything

to relieve his affliction, about which he could scarcely say anything. It became so bad that he even lost the power of speech and spent seven months unable to speak. He could not say mass, he could neither read, nor write, and could make hardly any movement without suffering extreme affliction. He could not even dress himself. All activity was forbidden him. He could neither converse with other people, nor listen to them, something that stemmed not from fatigue brought on as a result of his exorcism, but by the strange operation of the demons and the seizure of his faculties that rendered him practically incapable of anything. He did not preach and hardly heard any confessions and, when speech was denied him, he had to cease from all functions, which made him incapable of anything. He made tremendous efforts to resist, but it all seemed only to increase his sickness. He fell into an unknown sickness of which even the doctors knew nothing. Thus he was reduced to agony without being able to be helped by anyone.

In a letter written in the same year he said, 'My soul was like a palace with all the rooms closed and the bolts and padlocks fastened, leaving only the porter's room . . .'[19] His fellow-Jesuits thought him mad and treated him as such. One of them, Père Jacques Nau, has left a very hostile account of the Père Surin he knew:

Now Père Surin, whom I myself saw for twenty years or more, led a life so senseless and so shameful that one hardly dares speak of it. Finally it was such that the wisest attributed it all, and quite rightly, I believe, to madness; others saw there a diabolical possession, but wrongly, it seems to me, for nothing seemed to go beyond a natural mental illness, nor could the intervention of an external spirit be proved or demonstrated. So far as I know, he was never exorcized . . . I have no doubt that the quietists make much of it and would defend as one of their own this Père Surin whom, often, I have seen blaspheme the name of God and walk naked through the college, smeared with excrement – and I led him by the hand back to the infirmary. I have seen him beat himself with his fists and, for years, do a hundred other insanities, to the point of wanting to trample on the sacrament of the Eucharist – something I did not see myself, but heard of from witnesses the next day. He lived thus for many years. For the rest of his existence, he fulfilled no function in the Society. When he regained control of himself, he wrote books and letters, he visited his neighbour and spoke very well of God, but he never said his prayers, never recited his breviary, rarely celebrated mass and, up to his death, hopped about and gesticulated in a ridiculous and absurd fashion. In the last year of his life, dining with M. Du Sault in the presence of a numerous assembly, he threw a cup full of wine at the head of a serving girl. But those who were devoted to him were in ecstasies over it and found all that divine![20]

Much of this criticism – that he was mad, that he had brought it on himself (according to Père Nau by 'excessive reading of certain mystical authors')[21] – Surin himself accepted. He felt that his earnest search for God had been inspired by pride, and that his present state was proof that he was damned: 'It was a horrible disaster for me to see that, without thinking it, I had fallen into damnation.'[22] For fourteen years, from 1640 to 1653, we know hardly anything about Surin. At the college at Bordeaux he is simply a sick man, *infirmus*; there are hardly any letters; we have only glimpses of his life, hidden away in sickness and darkness. In May 1645 he seems to have tried to commit suicide by falling, or throwing himself, out of a window. He fell more than a hundred feet on to rocks on the banks of the river Garonne, but amazingly escaped with no more than a broken thigh. Thereafter he walked with a limp.

In 1654 the tide began to turn. On 14 September, the feast of the Exaltation of the Cross, Surin preached. That effort was followed by a period of depression, but none the less autumn that year saw a decided change in his condition, a ray of light in the shadows of his sickness. Autumn was often to be a time of renewal for Surin, a kind of recollection of the wonderful autumn when he was eight years old. But it doubtless had something to do with the wonderful season that autumn is in Bordeaux: in one place Certeau (a Bordelais himself, one guesses) remarks that 'the sumptuousness of autumn in Bordeaux authorizes every sort of rapture'.[23] But, despite his being on the mend, that sermon on Holy Cross day was an exception. Nor was he able to write – his correspondence remains fallow for several years yet – but he was now able to dictate, and from late 1654 onwards he began to compose some of his spiritual treatises – notably his *Catéchisme spirituel*, three volumes of which were complete by autumn 1655.

That autumn of 1655 saw a more decisive stage in his recovery. On 12 October he went to confession. He explained to the priest (the spiritual father of the college, Père Jean Ricard) that he felt himself to be damned. As he recalled it, eleven years later:

Although I was not in hell, I felt myself as damned as those who were. That was why the most dreadful of my crimes was to hope still and want to try to be good. And in fact, as our Lord permitted that I should bear the impressions of damnation, I felt the efforts that I made towards the good to be a real abomination, and I was rebuffed in them, in my opinion, by the power of God Himself and by the opposition of His divine being, which will wage war against the devil to all eternity. That rendered my wickedness quite deplorable and in such a state quite without remedy.

Père Ricard listened to Surin and then said that he had a secret he must tell him, although he was not at all a 'man of revelation': 'I have often had the impression that before you die our Lord will give you the grace to see that you are wrong and that you will come at last to act like other men, and I hope that you will die in peace.' These simple words made a strong impression on Surin. When his confessor had gone and he was left alone, Surin felt these words confirmed within his heart and he found himself able, little by little, to believe them. From that date, 12 October 1655, Surin counted the beginning of his healing. It was no sudden reversal, but a gradual recovery with many relapses. Only three days later, on the feast of St Teresa of Avila, a saint for whom Surin had a deep affection, he felt himself invaded by his old despair, and says that he would have committed suicide by throwing himself out of a window, had not his broken hip prevented him from getting up on to the sill. But still, from this moment, healing came to him 'like a day that comes to those who are in the shadow of the night . . . The dark sadness that had seized me went away only bit by bit, and serenity returned to my soul only by degrees'; or as he put it elsewhere, speaking of his soul as a palace that had been locked and barred: 'for four years, the Lord opened the doors and broke the padlocks, one after another'.[24]

For us, the idea of hell has so receded from our religious consciousness that the idea of being damned must seem very remote (though I suspect that such a conviction is less rare than we imagine). Surin's sense of being damned gripped him for years, and seemed to him to be the core of his black experience of madness and disorientation. In that age, however, such an experience was by no means unheard-of. In the 1580s St Francis de Sales had gone through a similar, though much briefer, experience.[25] Both of them came through this experience with a profound conviction of the universality of God's love that could not be restricted by a theology that envisaged that some were created to be damned.

In December 1657, in a letter to Jeanne des Anges, Surin talked to her about his gradual recovery, from 'two years ago' (the event just described) when 'our Lord put confidence into my soul with so much joy that now it seems to me that peace is almost completely established', through his experience at Pentecost in 1656 when 'an inundation of His love' covered all the evils that seemed to threaten him with perdition.[26]

From the beginning of that year, January 1657, Surin was able to write again and from that point on there flows the remarkable spiritual correspondence that marked the last years of his life. Again the recovery was gradual: there are thirteen letters for 1657, rising to over a hundred for 1661 (the yearly average is about fifty to sixty). The backbone of this correspondence consists of his letters to Jeanne des Anges (121 in all), which began with the letter just cited, written on 31 December 1657. Other significant correspondents include

Mme du Houx and the prioress of the Carmel at Bordeaux, Mère Jeanne de la Conception (Surin's letters to her are mostly addressed to the Carmel as a whole and constitute a series of reflections on the Carmelite vocation). We shall look at his spiritual teaching later, but from now on the existence of this correspondence, especially his letters to Jeanne des Anges, enables us to trace his life, and his inner life, in much more detail than hitherto. From this time onwards the sense of dereliction and disorientation was replaced by a conviction of God's love and a palpable sense of his grace. So much so that a disagreement arose between Surin and his confessor, now Père Bastide, as to what Surin's attitude should be to these 'consolations', this palpable sense of God's love and his grace. Bastide, following the teaching of St John of the Cross in the *Ascent of Mount Carmel*, advised Surin to reject these experiences and to rely on faith alone. Surin himself found that to reject such consolations did harm to his soul 'which, by this, found itself stripped of the grace that our Lord had given it and falling back into its natural poverty'.[27] He became convinced that it was not necessary or wise to reject such graces, only not to cling to them or to seek them out: as he puts it, 'God gives his graces to the soul for it to use them. He does not want this grace to take his place, or that one should resist it.'[28]

The disagreement runs on for months. Bastide ceases to be Surin's confessor. Surin discusses the whole matter with Jeanne des Anges who also discusses it with Bastide and cannot make up her mind whose side to take: she consults her guardian angel whose response is ambiguous, sphinx-like. It is an odd affair. On the one hand it reveals how much Surin wanted to confide in Jeanne des Anges and have her support: in one letter he says:

the soul having a certain need to expand and not being able to find true rest except in God, it is for me a kind of necessity to say something to a soul in which one finds God and towards which it can pour itself out according to his grace and the laws of his love.[29]

Surin found such a soul in the last years of his life in Jeanne des Anges, although in these years they never met. On the other hand, Surin's stress on the importance of not resisting the experience of grace places him not with St John of the Cross, who mistrusted such experiences, but with St Teresa of Avila, and other Christians such as John Wesley and St Symeon the New Theologian (to take such apparent extremes as an eighteenth-century Protestant and a tenth/eleventh-century Eastern Orthodox monk). In Surin's case, his emphasis on experience seems to be related to his experience of the desert in that the healing grace of God fell, for him, on an inner desert of such barrenness that to reject it would have been to refuse to acknowledge God's healing presence in his soul. It is interesting in this context to note that for Surin grace is not something *other than* God, something that could take God's place,[30] an idea that seems to lurk in some western theology and surfaces in Newman's famous hymn with its distinction between grace and 'a higher gift', which is 'God's presence and his very self', refined by 'flesh and blood' in the incarnation. Surin often calls God's presence in the soul grace, but lest we should think this anything less than God's very self, he very often, as we shall see, calls it the Holy Spirit, which could not be other than God himself.

The beginning of this ministry of correspondence was a sign of how far down the path of healing Surin had travelled, but it by no means marked its end. A further decisive step was taken in October 1660 when he recovered the use of his legs and was once again able to walk, look after himself, and eventually leave the infirmary, discard his status as *infirmus*, and take part once more in the communal life of the Jesuit college. In six months' time, he was even able to say mass. Although no one seems to have remarked on this, it seems to me that once he begins to say mass again, a new spirit enters his correspondence. Around Pentecost and the celebration ten days later of Corpus Christi (called in French, *le Fête-Dieu*), his letters are full of reflection on the transforming gift of the Holy Spirit, his descent as fire: 'the approach of this great feast . . . must set us all on fire, making us feel the warmth of the grace that was communicated to the apostles on this happy day'.[31] Three weeks later he writes more personally to Jeanne des Anges:

There is only one thing that is the life of my soul, and that is the inner conversation with our Lord, as gentle as I could hope for, and the discovery in this conversation of a most delightful employment and, in the warm experience of this love, of a very enjoyable occupation, in which the holy mass plays a great part which is for me like a bed of very gentle sleep . . . At this feast of Pentecost, our Lord has given me the grace to feel, it seems to me, the gentleness of His Spirit in a manner so penetrating and so surpassing one's ordinary ideas that it makes the soul beside itself so that it does not know whether to keep quiet or to speak, and there comes to me the word of our blessed Father John of the Cross who says to the soul whom God caresses and makes to feel his grace: 'O soul, say it to the world', and then takes it back, 'No, do not say it, for it cannot understand it.'[32]

This pattern is repeated each Pentecost and Corpus Christi thereafter. The stress on feelings and experiencing the Holy Spirit is made with very colourful language which it is hard to represent in English, and which draws especially on the sense of taste: the experience is *'savoureuse'* (at one point Surin speaks of the Holy Spirit as to be 'taken with the divine flesh like a marvellous sauce'!).[33]

As his strength grew, Surin began to preach again, and in the last couple of years of his life, he stomped around the Bordeaux countryside, visiting hospitals and villages and talking to all he met: 'I occupy myself in preaching to the people of the village [of Chelivettes] and going to see them in their little houses and talking to them with great happiness of the kingdom of God.'[34] By now he was, for his time, an old man. On 29 January 1665 Jeannes des Anges died (on what was, until recently, the feast of St Francis de Sales, canonized that year). Surin did not long survive her: he died on 21 April.

Much has already emerged of the significance of Père Surin as a 'desert father', whose desert was the extreme interior desolation of madness, which yet became fruitful by God's grace, bearing fruit especially in his ministry of spiritual direction. With some brief illustrations of this spiritual direction, we shall end this chapter.

It will be best, it seems to me, to illustrate Surin's spiritual teaching, not by trying to summarize it, which would rob it of the particularity of its epistolary form, but by developing some themes and giving some examples. One theme it seems obvious to discuss is that of the desert, which was not just an inner experience for Surin, but a focus for his reflections, especially in his letters to the Carmelites of Bordeaux. This latter fact reminds us that alongside the formative influence of Père Lallemant who directed his 'third year' (1629–30), Surin was deeply indebted to the Carmelite tradition. He regarded Isabelle des Anges, one of St Teresa's original disciples, as his spiritual mother, and remained in touch with the Carmel she founded in Bordeaux; he had read the works of the two Carmelite saints, often refers to his devotion to St Teresa, whose feast day in the middle of October fell in the autumn that was so often a period of renewal for him, and several times in his letters quotes from St John of the Cross, especially from his *Living Flame of Love*. It is in the letters to the Carmel at Bordeaux that the desert theme in his spirituality is most developed: 'Carmel is a desert. And it is not only evangelical poverty that makes its interior solitude; it is also the loftiness of this holy mountain which lifts its summit above the objects that can capture the human heart.'[35] The desert is empty, deprived of everything: so the interior desert is a state of 'perfect abnegation of all things'. This emphasis on self-emptying is one of the constant refrains in Surin's letters. As he himself says at one point: *'je n'ai qu'une chanson, de vider le coeur de tout'* ('I have only one song: empty the heart of everything').[36] Such radical self-emptying is very hard: we will cling to something, and often that something is our devotion itself – we can keep that, surely. In one of his letters Surin has this to say:

You must then seriously apply yourself to diminishing and weakening your efforts and your natural activity, in which you take a little contentment and a little satisfaction, thinking that this work pleases God. He is not so pleased with it as you think, my dear daughter, and although your diligence does please Him, He would be even more pleased if we were to listen to Him and let Him act. It would seem that there is nothing so easy to do as this, however I find very few people who listen to Him and I see many who feed on feelings to which they have contributed and prefer them to this delicate peace that is in the depths of the heart (*'au fond du coeur'*), because it is less palpable, though much more powerful.[37]

In one of his letters to the Carmel at Bordeaux, he singles out our own activity as one of the 'tumults' (along with unnecessary conversation and disordered passions) that prevent the sisters entering the desert of Carmel, 'the true desert to which our souls ought to retreat, which is God: the desert where are to be found perfect silence, solid peace, and the abundance of all goods':

> The third tumult that troubles the silence of the soul is that of our own activity. For although the soul must be diligent to please God and must exercise itself in acts of virtue, it nevertheless often happens to people of your calling that, God wanting to put them in entire dependence on his grace and to subject their faculties wholly to Himself, He assumes the right to make them attentive to His word. Then they must make the tumult of their own needs and operations cease, not so as to throw themselves into an indiscreet and cheating laziness, which is the desert and lair of the devil, but so as to be more submissive to the leading of the Holy Spirit and to give Him the freedom to dispose of them as he wills. For this divine Spirit is only ever pleased when He does in the soul what He wills; and for that, the soul must abandon itself wholly to Him, whether to act or to suffer, according to His holy will.

And Surin concludes: 'Here is what the silence of the divine desert properly consists of: the soul, recollected and tranquil, lets God act, without disturbing the divine operation by the tumult of its own activity.'[38]

One enters the desert by emptying one's heart of everything. But we would misunderstand Surin if we read this as meaning that we are to cultivate an attitude of bleak indifference to created things. Surin himself, we have seen, was not

119

so indifferent: the beautiful autumns of the Guyenne were often times of grace and renewal for him. It is not indifference that Surin counsels, rather a freedom from attachment, or, put another way, the cultivation of an attitude of receptiveness. In another of his letters to Carmel he says:

> the solitude and abandonment of worldly and human things must be the garden in which your heart walks. Not that there is anything attractive about solitude in itself, because it is only a vacuum, but much more that this solitude is filled with God who, in His majesty, greatness, beauty and goodness, completely occupies it and thus makes it a place of intercourse for the souls of Carmel.[39]

'The desert shall rejoice and blossom,' said the prophet Isaiah (Isa. 35:1): that is Surin's desert, and it rejoices and blossoms not because of any natural fecundity – it has none, otherwise it would not be a desert – but because God makes this desert a garden. And for Surin this is all underwritten by his own experience of the utter desolation of his mind blossoming and rejoicing under the hand of God.

Surin's teaching on the desert encompasses both his own awesome experience and a very simple message about our approaching God free from the human clutter that we are so prone to bring along. In an early letter he wrote to a nun, Anne Buignon:

> As for your prayer, I regard it in no way as a bad sign that you say that you cannot hold your mind to any subject in particular that you have prepared. I advise you never to tie yourself to a subject, but to go to prayer with the same freedom of heart as you would go into the room of Mère d'Arrérac [Anne's mother superior] to talk to her and to help her pass the time. You do not take with you three or four prepared points of conversation: that would hinder the pleasantness of your conversation. You go with a general disposition to cultivate your friendship. Go to God in the same way, something that does not prevent you having some mystery in mind, but without tying down your mind.[40]

Surin's teaching sometimes seems hard and uncompromising – and he had hard things to say about those who would soften the severity of the gospel[41] – but he is unwilling to compromise, lest we deceive ourselves and remain in a world that is no more than a human construct, and fail to go out into the desert where we can receive and experience the riches of God's healing love.

NOTES

Fundamental for any study of Père Jean-Joseph Surin is Michel de Certeau SJ's edition of his correspondence (with a preface by Julien Green, Bibliothèque Européenne, Paris, 1966). Certeau has also edited Surin's *Guide spirituel* (Collection Christ, no. 12, Paris, 1963). Both of these have valuable introductions by Certeau, and in the case of the *Correspondance* invaluable notes and commentary. Henri Bremond wrote on Surin and Jeanne des Anges in his monumental *Histoire Littéraire du Sentiment Religieux en France*, vol. 5 (1926), pp. 148–310. In English there is Aldous Huxley, *The Devils of Loudun* (London, 1952) and, more important, a chapter in John Saward, *Perfect Fools* (Oxford, 1980), pp. 118–46 (notes, pp. 234–6).

1 Letter 289 (11.ii.1660), *Correspondance*, p. 919.
2 Bremond, p. 152.
3 ibid. p. 159.
4 Letter 356 (mid-iii.1661), *Correspondance*, p. 1084; and see Certeau's introd., pp. 42–51.
5 Letter 320 (28.ix.1660), ibid. p. 996.
6 In his *Science Expérimentale*, quoted in ibid. p. 996.
7 For Père Lallemant, see *Christian Spirituality*, vol. 3, ed. L. Dupré and D. E. Saliers (London, 1990), pp. 53–63; Bremond, pp. 3–65; Saward, pp. 104–17.
8 Bremond, p. 186.
9 *Correspondance*, pp. 244 f.
10 Keith Thomas, *Religion and the Decline of Magic* (London, 1971), p. 492.
11 Bremond, p. 218.
12 Appendix II, *Correspondance*, pp. 1721–48.
13 Prof. E. de Greef, 'Succédanés et concomitances psychologiques de la "Nuit obscure" ' in *Etudes Carmélitaines* 23 (1938), II, 163 f, quoted in ibid. p. 1733.

The Wilderness of God

14   From Surin's *Triomphe de l'amour divin*, quoted by Bremond, pp. 198 f.
15   See the ch. in Charles Williams, *He Came Down from Heaven* (London, 1950), pp. 82–94.
16   See *Correspondance*, pp. 270 f.
17   See ibid. p. 563 and cf. p. 324.
18   See ibid. pp. 424–30, and Bremond, pp. 242–51.
19   For both passages see *Correspondance*, pp. 423 f; the letter (315: 25.viii.1660) appears in full on pp. 983 f.
20   Quoted in ibid. pp. 481 f.
21   ibid. p. 483.
22   In Surin's *Science Expérimentale*, quoted in ibid. p. 433.
23   ibid. p. 844.
24   For this see ibid. pp. 514–16, and for the final quotation, letter 315 (25.viii.1660), p. 984.
25   See *Christian Spirituality*, vol. 3, p. 563.
26   Letter 158 (31.xii.1657), *Correspondance*, p. 563.
27   From his *Science Expérimentale*, quoted in ibid. p. 520.
28   ibid. p. 764.
29   Letter 327 (17.xi.1660), ibid. p. 1018.
30   See note 28.
31   Letter 380 (Beginning-vi. 1661), *Correspondance*, p. 1138.
32   Letter 387 (27.vi.1661), ibid. pp. 1156–8.
33   ibid. p. 1158.
34   Letter 469 (26.vi.1662), ibid. p. 1399.
35   Letter 225 (19.iii.1659), ibid. pp. 762 f.
36   Letter 324 (ix-x.1660?), ibid. p. 1005.
37   Letter 114 (17.ii.1658), ibid. p. 577.
38   Letter 217 (3.iii.1659), ibid. pp. 736–9.
39   Letter 467 (23.vi.1662), ibid. p. 1391.
40   Letter 94 (21.ix.1636), ibid. p. 351.
41   See letter 268 (Beginning-xii.1659), ibid. p. 870.

7

The Russian Desert: The Forest

In some Russian icons of St John the Forerunner (John the Baptist), the saint is depicted not against the background of a rocky, sandy desert with the occasional juniper bush, but of a dense *forest*.[1] For in the Russian experience the dense, inhospitable forest, the *taiga*, played the role that the desert had played for Christians in the fourth century. It was into the forest that monks and ascetics withdrew for solitude and prayer; it was the forest that represented that part of the earth that was hostile to human settlement. In his famous book, *The Russian Religious Mind*, George Fedotov argued that the experience of the desert or forest belonged, not to the first phase of Russian Christianity that was centred on Kiev after the conversion of Prince Vladimir (or Volodimer) in (traditionally) 988, but to the next stage of Russian history, after the Mongol invasion (1237–40) and the razing of Kiev to the ground in 1242:

> The new monastic asceticism, which can be dated from the second quarter of the fourteenth century, is essentially different from that of Ancient Russia. It is the monasticism of the 'desert'. All the known monasteries of Kievan Russia were built in towns or suburbs of towns. Most of them survived the pillage of Baty or were later restored like the Monastery of the Caves in Kiev, but the disappearance of the ideal of personal sanctity betokens an inner decay. Urban monasteries were still built during Mongol times, for example, in Moscow. Yet, most of the saints of the age left the towns for the virgin forest. We can only conjecture as to the actual motives of this new trend in the monastic

movement. One possible explanation is that it reflects the difficult and turbulent life in the cities, which were still subject to occasional devastation by new Tatar raids. On the other hand, however, the very decadence of the urban monastic houses prompted the zealous to search for new ways, ways that were already indicated in the classical tradition of the desert monasticism of Egypt and Syria. Russia did not have any 'desert' in the literal sense, but monks still could escape both men and civilization: the vast Northern *forest* thus became the 'desert' of the Russian monks. In their fervent choice of the wilderness these pioneers revealed a greater detachment from the world and its destinies than the monks of Kiev . . . But, still, in taking upon themselves the harder task – one necessarily connected with contemplative prayer – they elevated spiritual life to a height not yet achieved in Russia.[2]

If Fedotov is right, then the history of Christianity in Russia superficially echoes the history of Christianity itself: first, an urban phenomenon, and then a retreat into the desert. But the echo is only superficial: for the fourth-century flight into the desert was a reaction to the establishment of Christian society, whereas the fourteenth-century search for the forest was a flight from a disintegrating society; further, we are witnessing in such a search for the desert a change in monasticism itself, from established urban monasticism to a renewal of the quest for the desert, rather than the discovery of monasticism itself. But it may be that Fedotov overdraws the contrast between Kievan monasticism and monasticism after the Mongol invasion. There are, as he admits, not many sources for the Kievan period, and the most important of these – the *Paterik* (the lives of the fathers) of the Kievan Caves Monastery – does somewhat belie the contrast. For, though the Monastery of the Caves was (and is) situated in the city of Kiev, the accounts of its origins suggest that what was sought was a place remote from human society. It is related in the *Paterik* that Ilarion who later, in 1051, became Metropolitan of Kiev, 'used to go from Berstovo to a hill above the Dnieper, where the old Caves Monastery now is, and pray, for there was a thick wood there. Here he dug a small cave, fourteen feet deep': that cave was used by Antonij who founded the Caves Monastery.[3] However that is to be interpreted, it seems to want to suggest that the inspiration of the Caves Monastery was a place of retreat, hidden away in the woods. The very form of the *Paterik* (from the Greek *Paterikon*) also suggests the inspiration of the Desert Fathers, the subjects of the original Greek *Paterikon*. At least when the *Paterik* was compiled, from earlier sources in the fourteenth century, the monks of the Caves Monastery were regarded as a Russian version of the fathers of the Egyptian desert.

Whatever else all this implies, it certainly means that Kievan monasticism saw itself as inheriting a tradition, the tradition of the Desert Fathers and their successors in the Gaza desert, especially as reflected in the greatest eastern work on the monastic life, the *Ladder* of St John of Sinai.[4] Yet the *Paterik* itself seems to reflect a very imperfect form to this ideal. As Muriel Heppell remarks in the introduction to her translation of the *Paterik*, 'we see that many of the monks are depicted as lazy, avaricious, quarrelsome, disobedient, worldly . . . and prone to spiritual pride'. She continues:

> In fact, the paradox contains an important spiritual truth, for in common is a steadfast determination to 'try again' after every fall. There are two words, both difficult to translate adequately into English, which occur frequently in the *Paterik*: *podvig* and *ispravlenie*. The former usually denotes the successful performance of a difficult task or progress achieved as a result of strenuous effort, while the latter, which means literally 'correction', indicates a continual and indeed unending process of 'amending one's life' and self-improvement which was the monk's primary task . . . The frank description of the sins and weakness of fallible human beings and the often dramatic narrative of the intense struggle waged by individuals to conquer their faults make the *Paterik* far more convincing as a work designed to help those living the monastic life, than if it had presented only tales of virtue and sanctity. It is a chronicle of steadfast spiritual endeavour. As such, it has enduring validity . . . [5]

The juxtaposition of *podvig* (which can often take the form of
the dictionary definition as 'heroic deed') and *ispravlenie*
(which is often a humdrum 'trying to do better next time')
perhaps points to a holding together of extremes to the point
of paradox that seems – if one dare generalize – characteristi-
cally, if not peculiarly, Russian. Another example might be
a justice carried to the point of cruelty combined with an
apparently whimsical mercy, in which the claims of justice
and charity are accepted without there being any attempt to
reconcile them in something reasonable: something that can
possibly be seen in the life of Tsar Ivan 'the Terrible'. Perhaps
this Russian sense of paradox finds its literary climax at the
end of the legend of the Grand Inquisitor in Dostoevsky's
The Brothers Karamazov when Christ responds to the Grand
Inquisitor's speech by saying nothing but instead giving him
a kiss.

Fedotov traces the Russian spirituality of the forest from
St Sergius of Radonezh, through what he calls the 'Thebaid
of the North' – monasteries such as the 'White Lake' founded
by St Cyril of Belozersk ('of the White Lake'), another one
nearby founded by Cyril's companion, St Ferapont, Obnora
(founded by St Paul, who called silence the mother of all
virtues) and the Solovets monastery on an island in the White
Sea – to St Nil of Sora and the 'non-possessors' (those monks
who rejected even the acquisition of communal property by
monks). He saw this tradition continued in the eighteenth and
nineteenth centuries in St Tikhon of Zadonsk, St Seraphim of
Sarov and the famous monastery, close to Moscow, called
Optina Pustyn – the desert of Optino (Fedotov's *Russian
Religious Mind* does not go beyond the fifteenth century, but
his anthology, *A Treasury of Russian Spirituality*, makes it clear
how he saw this tradition continuing).

This tradition of the Russian spirituality of the forest, which
Fedotov associates especially with the monastic tradition of
the 'non-possessors', saw the forest, the desert, as a place of
spiritual experience, and also a source of spiritual wisdom, in
much the same way as we have seen in the case of the Desert
Fathers. When we read the lives of these Russian saints, there
is a strong sense that we are breathing the same spiritual
atmosphere as the early fathers of the desert. Part of the

reason for this is that Russia received Christianity from the Byzantine Greeks and never lost the sense that the origins of its tradition lay with the Greeks. Two illustrations of this can be given in the lives of St Sergius of Radonezh and St Paissy Velichkovsky.

St Sergius of Radonezh revived Russian monasticism during the period of the triumph in the Byzantine East of the doctrine and spirituality of hesychasm (St Sergius lived *c.* 1314–92; hesychasm was vindicated at councils held in Constantinople in 1347 and 1351). The focus of links between Russia and the Byzantine East – then as later – was the Greek peninsula, east of Thessalonika, entirely given over to monastic settlements, called the Holy Mountain of Athos: and it was the Holy Mountain that was the centre of hesychasm. What was 'hesychasm'? The name derives from a Greek word, *hesychia*, which means stillness or silence, something that has always been seen as the aim of the monastic life: a stillness and silence in which prayer and attention to God becomes possible. More particularly, hesychasm refers to an understanding of interior prayer in which the whole of the human person becomes so receptive of God that it is deified, transfigured by and into the divine, and in this experience beholds the Godhead as a transfiguring light. The experience of the disciples on the Mount of the Transfiguration is seen as foreshadowing the experience of any Christian (and especially any monk) who attains to inward prayer in which the whole of one's being is absorbed, what is called 'prayer of the heart': 'When you were transfigured on the mountain, Christ God, you showed your disciples your glory, so far as they were able. Shed your eternal light on us sinners also, at the prayers of the Mother of God. Giver of Light, glory to You' (*apolytikion* for the feast of the Transfiguration). To defend the reality of this experience of transfiguration in the divine light in which we become God, St Gregory Palamas developed his doctrine (drawing on hints found in earlier theologians) of the distinction in God between the divine essence, which remains ineffable, and the divine energies, that can be experienced: this doctrine was much contested, but was confirmed at the councils of 1347 and 1351. Another distinctive feature of hesychasm in this limited sense is its teaching on the use of the 'Jesus Prayer' in seeking the prayer of the heart. This prayer – usually: 'O Lord Jesus Christ, Son of God, have mercy upon me, a sinner' – is gently repeated as a way of overcoming distraction and attaining prayer of the heart.

Fedotov points out what he calls an 'inner affinity' between Sergius' inner life and hesychasm, and is clearly inclined to believe that hesychasm exercised some influence on him.[6] Whether or not that is the case, it is certainly likely that Sergius' disciples were influenced by the spirituality emanating from the Holy Mountain.[7]

If in the case of Sergius and his disciples the influence of hesychasm can be regarded as evidence of Russia's continued indebtedness to Byzantine spirituality, the same sense of Greek monastic experience as the well from which the renewal of Russian spiritual life could draw is seen even more strongly in the case of St Paissy Velichkovsky. Paissy was born in Poltava in the Ukraine in 1722.[8] He belonged to a priestly family and the expectation was that he would, in turn, become a priest and serve in Poltava. To this end he went to Kiev for his education. But by the time he was sixteen he was convinced that he wanted to become a monk and left Kiev and began his wanderings in search of a spiritual father and the life of a monk. His wanderings eventually took him to Mount Athos where he stayed for seventeen years, and soon established himself as the leader of a skete of Wallachian and Slavic monks, who devoted themselves to the prayer of the heart. To begin with they settled at the St Constantine Skete and later restored and moved to the Skete of the Prophet Elijah, both sketes dependencies of the Monastery of the Pantocrator on the northern side of the peninsula. It was on the Holy Mountain that Paissy discovered the tradition of hesychasm, and its literature – the writings of St Gregory of Sinai and St Gregory Palamas, St Symeon the New Theologian, St Diadochus, St Hesychius and others – a literature that was by Paissy's own account[9] neglected even on the Holy Mountain (as by the eighteenth century spoken Greek had become far removed from the written Greek of the Fathers), and was largely untranslated into Slavonic. For the rest of his life Paissy devoted himself to making this spiritual treasury available to the Slavonic world. Perhaps the most influential of these translations was his (partial) Slavonic translation of the collection of hesychast texts made by St Nicodemus of the Holy Mountain and St Macarius of Corinth called the *Philokalia*.[10] Not that he spent the rest of his days peacefully on the Holy Mountain. The Holy Mountain was not a peaceful place, subject as it was to harassment by the Turks, and so in 1763 Paissy left Mount Athos and with his monks travelled to Moldavia (now divided between Romania and the Moldavian Republic), first to found a monastery at Dragomirna, from which he moved first to Sekul and finally to Niamets, where he died in 1794. Paissy's presence in Moldavia was critically important for the revival of monasticism in the whole of the Slavonic world: through his disciples his influence spread beyond Moldavia into Russia and was felt in the Solovetsk monastery, at Valaam and in the St Alexander Nevsky Lavra, at Optina Pustyn, and many other places.

The story of the revival of monasticism in Russia from the late eighteenth century onwards is mainly the story of the spread of Paissy's influence, of the spread of a monasticism that centred on the prayer of the heart achieved through the Jesus Prayer, and of the revival of the institution of spiritual fatherhood, called in Russia *starchestvo* (from *staretz*, an elder). But already, independently of Paissy, the Russian forest was drawing men to a life of solitude and stillness, as can be seen from the example of St Tikhon and others.

St Tikhon was born Timothy Sokolov in 1724 in the village of Korotzk, in the diocese of Novgorod.[11] He belonged to a 'clerical' family – his father was the village sexton – but his father died when he, the youngest of six children, was young. The family was extremely poor, and it was at home that he learnt to read and write. He was fourteen by the time he went to school in Novgorod, at great sacrifice to his family, especially his elder brothers. Two years later in 1740 he entered the seminary at Novgorod. Despite his late start he made good progress and in 1751 was appointed teacher of Greek at the seminary, while his studies were still continuing. At this stage he could have married and become a parish priest, or continued to teach (teachers were in much demand: Moscow University was founded in 1755), but he was drawn to solitude and the monastic life. Years later he told one of his companions about an experience he had when he was a teacher, that had shown him where his heart was being drawn:

> When I was still a teacher, I had formed the habit . . . of spending the night without sleep, either reading or meditating . . . This night in the month of May was very pleasant, mild and light. I left my room and went out on to the porch, which was on the north side, and standing there I meditated on eternal bliss. Suddenly the skies opened and were filled with a glow and a dazzling light such as mortal tongue is unable to describe: the mind is quite incapable of grasping it. This lasted but a moment, and then the skies regained their ordinary appearance, while I, who had beheld this wondrous vision, conceived an ardent desire to lead a life of solitude. And for a long time afterwards my mind recalled what I had seen, and even now, when I think of it, my heart is filled with joy and happiness.[12]

In her fine study of St Tikhon, Nadejda Gorodetsky remarks on this vision: 'Love for Nature and beauty; retirement; the thought of eternity; and joy – these gave a clear premonition of the spiritual path which was opening before St Tikhon'.[13]

In 1758 Timothy Sokolov became a monk and was given the name of Tikhon. He was soon ordained deacon and priest, and found himself, now a monk, still engaged in teaching – philosophy now. The next year he was appointed archimandrite (abbot) of the Zheltikov monastery in the diocese of Tver (south of Novgorod). The following year he was appointed rector of the seminary at Tver and head of the Otroch monastery. The year after that he found himself elected Bishop of Keksholm and Ladoga, as a suffragan to the Archbishop of Novgorod. Two years later he was nominated Bishop of Voronezh, on the river Don in the south of Russia, in the country of the Cossacks. Tikhon spent four years there, educating and inspiring his clergy and people, but by now his strength was exhausted and he was often ill. At the end of 1767 he resigned and retired to a monastery, eventually to the monastery of Zadonsk on a tributary of the Don, after which it was named. There he spent fourteen years in an obscure monastery, dogged by ill-health and bouts of depression, in the solitude that had been denied him for so long.

St Tikhon is one who was drawn to the desert as a place of solitude and prayer, attracted by its beauty, but only found his way there through physical sickness and ill-health, after strenuously serving the Church as a teacher, pastor and administrator. It is possibly this that explains his emphasis on the Christian teaching on humility and dependence on God:

> God descends to the humble as waters flow down from the hills into the valleys. God creates out of nothing; and if we sincerely recognize ourselves as being nothing, he will recreate our hearts. This new creation . . . produces as it were a ceaseless hunger and thirst after the grace of God; for humility does not consider what it already possesses but seeks what it has not yet . . . Humility is a learning compared with self-satisfied ignorance; for one who learns in this school of divine wisdom, the more he partakes of divine gifts the better he sees his spiritual misery and, out of real want, he seeks in sighing. The lonely path of humility leads men to the Highest.[14]

Similarly his attitude to temptation is less that it provides an opportunity for spiritual combat, than that it is something that assists self-knowledge: 'it is like an emetic, it reveals what there is inside us.'[15] And what there is inside us are various strategies to bolster up our self-esteem and set ourselves up over against others. Tikhon warns against pride, irritability, a tendency to judge others: what he says about how to cope with a hot temper seems to have a very personal accent:

> If by nature or habit you are inclined to get angry, take care to avoid anything which excites in you this passion. Calm yourself even though only for a short while, and count how many days you have passed without being cross. Supposing that you are in the habit of getting irritable

every day; well, if for the whole day, or for two or for three, you have not been angry, it is a sign that your anger is diminishing. If you see that a whole week has passed thus, go to church, and fervently thank your creator for such a mercy . . . And what if I manage to do this for five, six weeks at a time?[16]

In his retreat in Zadonsk, Tikhon became known and sought after as a spiritual father, a *staretz:* much of his counsel and direction survives in letters, as well as in the various books that he wrote. Unusually (though in this like his Greek contemporary St Nicodemus of the Holy Mountain who compiled the *Philokalia*) he drew not just on Orthodox – Russian and Greek – sources for his inspiration, but also on western sources: he possessed works by the German pietist Johannes Arndt and the Anglican bishop Joseph Hall. He was perhaps drawn to them because he shared with the West a devotion to Christ in his humanity and his suffering:

Remember, often, especially during the night, the suffering of Christ. It will kindle in you love for the Sufferer; this love will preserve you from sin. Meditate upon His Passion: it helps the fulfilment of Christian duty . . . The suffering of Christ is like a saving book from which we learn all the supreme Good: repentance, faith, devotion to God, love of our neighbour, humility, meekness, patience, detachment from worldly vanities; like a spur it stimulates one.[17]

'Especially during the night': Tikhon was fond of praying by night, his early vision occurred then, he often commends meditation 'at night': here on the passion, elsewhere on eternity.[18] The night, as we have seen, is the daily 'desert-time'. The yearly season answering to the desert is winter, especially in Russia and other northern countries, where the contrast of the seasons is more marked. Some of Tikhon's meditations draw on the contrast of the seasons, especially the contrast between winter and spring:

Winter has come, the earth is covered with snow, frost has chained lakes, rivers and marshes, and thus a free road has been made so that there is no longer any need for bridges and other means of crossing. This is divine benevolence, serving your need: bless him who gives snow (Ps: 148:8). Winter passes and spring approaches. You can regard this as a resurrection of all nature which died by frost: bless him who thus appointed it. Spring has burst out; it reveals a new treasury of divine gifts; the sun shines and warms pleasantly, the air is filled with scents; the womb of the earth brings forth its riches; the fruit of seeds and roots appears and offers itself for the use of all; the meadows, the cornfields, the woods deck themselves with green, they adorn themselves with flowers and pour out fragrance; the springs flow and the impetuosity of rivers gladdens not the sight alone but also the hearing; everywhere the diverse voices of a variety of birds make sweet melody; the cattle stray over the meadows and steppes, no longer asking food from us but fed and satisfied with what the hand of God spreads before them – they eat and play as though thanking God for his mercies; in a word, all things under heaven change into a new, beautiful and gladsome form; both animate and inanimate creation is so to speak born anew.[19]

The desert of winter creates a 'free road', along which we journey towards spring which is the 'time of gifts'. Spring speaks to Tikhon in much the same way as autumn spoke to Père Surin. In both their joy in nature is an aspect of their receptiveness to God. For both prayer is longing for God and the delight of being in his presence and sharing his gifts. For both the life-blood of the Christian is prayer: 'as a bird without wings, as a soldier without arms, so is a Christian without prayer,' says Tikhon,[20] prayer that can be made:

at all times, in all places, by the mind and the spirit. You can lift up your mind and heart to God while walking, sitting, working, in the crowd and in solitude. His door is always open, unlike man's. We can always say to him in our hearts: Lord! Lord! have mercy![21]

Somewhat younger than Tikhon, but still largely independent of the tradition that stemmed from St Paissy, was St Seraphim

of Sarov.[22] A native of central Russia, he became a monk at
the monastery of Sarov, on a hill, the site of an ancient fort,
covered with dense forest. He was then nineteen. He served
his novitiate and was ordained deacon and then priest. After
sixteen years in the monastery he withdrew into the surrounding forest where he lived alone a life of extreme asceticism,
eating very sparingly (for a three-year period he is said to
have lived on nothing but ground elder),[23] and spending his
time in prayer or working in his vegetable garden. In this
period he spent times echoing in his own life the ancient
'pillar saints' like St Symeon Stylites: he would spend all
night standing on a rock repeating 'God, be merciful to me,
a sinner'. During these years he experienced temptations and
anxieties that almost reduced him to despair, but also knew
periods of delight in the assurance of God's love. 'He who
has chosen the hermit life,' he said:

> must feel himself constantly crucified . . . The hermit,
> tempted by the spirit of darkness, is like dead leaves chased
> by the wind, like clouds driven by the storm; the demon
> of the desert bears down on the hermit at about midday
> and sows restless worries in him, and distressing desires as
> well. These temptations can only be overcome by prayer.[24]

But he also said:

> When mind and heart are united in prayer, without any
> distraction, you feel that spiritual warmth which comes
> from Christ and fills the whole inner being with joy and
> peace . . . We have to withdraw from the visible world so
> that the light of Christ can come down into our heart.
> Closing our eyes, concentrating our attention on Christ,
> we must try to unite our mind with the heart and, from
> the depths of our whole being, we must call on the Name
> of our Lord, saying: 'Lord, Jesus Christ, have mercy upon
> me, a sinner.'[25]

After fifteen years of this solitary existence in the forest, during
which time his health was weakened – partly owing to the
life itself, partly as the result of an attack by brigands who

thought he must be guarding some treasure – Seraphim returned to his monastery in May 1810.

Back in the monastery Seraphim continued his solitary life, now by keeping to his cell and only emerging at night for a brief walk. In 1815 he began to break his seclusion and opened his door to occasional visitors. Those who visited him found that he had remarkable powers of spiritual intuition; many experienced healing, both physical and spiritual. Soon thousands were coming from all over Russia to visit Seraphim and consult him. The recluse had become a *staretz*. Among his spiritual children the nuns of the nearby monastery of Diveyevo had a special place: in the last years of his life Seraphim took a much more personal interest in their welfare, reorganized their life, and saw to the building of a new monastic complex, including a church.

Seraphim is perhaps the most striking example of a life of extreme asceticism and seclusion forming the preparation for the gift of spiritual fatherhood. In Seraphim's case recourse to him as a spiritual father extended beyond his earthly life, which ended in 1833. After his death there were many stories – especially at Diveyevo – of visions of him bringing advice and the comfort of his presence at critical times. Seraphim himself seems to have envisaged and even intended this:

> When I am no longer with you, come to my grave. Whenever you have the time, come, the more often the better. Whatever you have on your mind, whatever happened to you, come to me, and bring whatever sorrow you have with you to my grave. Fall down on the earth, as you would to someone living, and tell me all there is to tell, and I shall hear you, all your sorrows will fly away and pass. As you always spoke to the living person, so also here. For I am alive and shall be for ever.[26]

In this Seraphim shows his faith in the risen Christ who 'by death trampled on death and to those in the graves gave life'.

If in St Tikhon and St Seraphim we see the desert tradition of inward prayer and spiritual fatherhood that Paissy's labours of translation and example sought to feed, in the monastery of Optina Pustyn – the desert of Optino – we see

Paissy's direct influence bearing fruit. Optino was near to Moscow and was visited by intellectuals from the city, who drew on this living experience of Orthodox hesychasm and gave it wider currency. Perhaps the most important intellectual contact with Optino was Ivan Kireevsky, the Slavophil, who collaborated with the monastery in the publication of Paissy's translations. Certainly the best-known visitors were the novelists Leo Tolstoy and Fyodor Dostoevsky. Dostoevsky spent the inside of three days there in 1878; his encounter with the *staretz* Amvrosy provided some of the inspiration for his account of the *staretz* Zossima in *The Brothers Karamazov*.

St Amvrosy himself is another example of a Russian desert – or forest – father.[27] He was born in 1812 and was educated at the seminary at Tambov, where he was a brilliant pupil. Like Tikhon, his sensitivity to nature played a part in his realization of his monastic vocation. After leaving the seminary, while he was working as a teacher, he was walking in the woods beside the river Voronezh. When he stopped and listened, he thought he heard the river sounding 'Praise God! Keep God!' (*Hvalite Boga! Hranite Boga!*): 'I stood there for a long time,' he later recalled, 'I listened to the mysterious voice of nature and was greatly astonished by it.'[28] In 1839 he went to Optino and in 1840 became a monk. By 1846 he was helping the *staretz* Makary in the work of spiritual direction and from 1865 – after Makary's death and the death of the monastery's abbot Moisei – he became the sole *staretz* at Optino. Like Tikhon, he suffered from poor health, and this physical weakness, in a way, protected his seclusion. Like Seraphim, towards the end of his life he was much occupied in providing for a convent of nuns, in this case at Shamordino, near to Optino. Like both of them he was much sought after as a spiritual director. His teaching is much in line with theirs. Like them, it was essentially personal, addressed to particular situations into which he showed great insight, and thus lends itself with difficulty to summarization. In some contrast to them (though this should not be exaggerated), his teaching is more deeply influenced by the forms and doctrines of hesychast spirituality. In this he is more like his contemporaries St Ignaty Brianchaninov and St Theophan the Recluse (both of whom were canonized at the same time as St

Amvrosy and St Paissy – on the occasion of the millenium of Russian Christianity in 1988), both of whom made trans-lations of the *Philokalia* into Russian (rather than Paissy's Slavonic) and wrote much expounding the hesychast spiritu-ality of the prayer of the heart.

Even when he was weary and exhausted, Amvrosy agreed to see people and talk with them, and even in such a state his comments lost none of their sharpness, or their humour, as the following extract from the diary of a woman who visited him shows:

This evening [the day before she was to leave] when it was already quite late the father asked me to come for a farewell talk. He was terribly tired and was lying down when I came to him . . . I unwittingly remarked to him that many disturb him with trifles and that in general he is too occu-pied with external matters. Even, I said, those persons who are constantly with him, a holy *staretz*, are little permeated by an inward, spiritual life. To his question who these people were I named two. 'And how do you know?' he asked. 'One can feel it,' I answered. 'One is more of a busybody, but envy is common to both. We, although we are sinners, would sooner lay down our lives for others than would they.' 'But perhaps they have such a hidden goodness as redeems all their other faults, a goodness which you do not see,' he answered. 'In you there is a great ability to sacrifice, but the Lord said, "I desire mercy and not sacrifice." And you have little mercy; that is why you judge everyone without condescension. You look only at the bad side of a man and do not look at his good side; but you do see your own sacrifices and exalt yourself because of them.' To my words that I would like to live close to him, the *staretz* directly and at the same time compassionately sent a reproach straight to my heart with the words: 'No, better far away. Or you will begin to judge the *staretz* also for not doing as you think right.'[29]

Practice of the Jesus Prayer was very much a part of the spirituality that St Amvrosy imparted, but he was acutely aware of the dangers that arise when this prayer (or any prayer) is used as a technique without the guidance of a spiritual father. To a nun he once wrote:

> You have become so carried away with your own reasoning and sense of worth that, disdaining counsel and acting on your own, you arrived, as it were, at self-moving prayer of the heart during your sleep. This happens to a few rare holy people who have achieved extreme purification from passions. But those who are still subject to passions should hearken to what one man informed us. Listening in a half-sleep to a similar movement to the one you described, he paid close attention and what did he hear? He heard a cat's *meow* cunningly pronounced in a way similar to the words of the prayer. Sister! We must humble ourselves. Our stature is still very small . . . [30]

These deserts of the spirit did not survive the Russian Revolution: Optino was closed in 1923, Sarov in 1927 (Seraphim's relics were exhumed and removed, destined to be an exhibit in a Museum of Atheism). And yet perhaps they did: in a hideous caricature that has yet been spiritually fruitful. As one begins to read Alexander Solzhenitsyn's *Gulag Archipelago*, one is startled to notice that one of the prison camps was at Solovki, part of Fedotov's 'Thebaid of the North'.

Iulia de Beausobre, who was arrested in Moscow in 1932 and interrogated in the infamous Lyubyanka, but miraculously survived, told of a vision she had, shortly before she left Russia when she was nursing the sick in a lumber camp south-east of Moscow:

> Straight ahead, beyond the pale streak of the fence, a pitch-black giant fir tree leapt towards us stretching far up into the steaming sky; shafts of rays like moonlight shot out of it, throwing into relief great downward-sweeping ribs of various grey – the branches. The light seemed to issue from inside the tree, but the trunk remained velvet dark. Could it be the sun rising behind? We faced east, but miles of tousled thicket blocked the way between tree and sun. 'Father Seraphim!' exclaimed Kilina in a rapture, 'a mark

of pity, of comfort for you and me from him; given to us through a redeemed creature, a redeemed tree!'[31]

At the same time she came to know a Russian nun, also consigned to this lumber camp, who was dying. For her too Seraphim's presence was palpable:

> Be comforted, for we are in the care of Seraphim of the Holy Woods, the intercessor for all who suffer here. Infinite is our joy, incomplete only because our brothers beyond the distant border do not deign to understand what it is God wants of us and what it is we want of them. Only that they should keep burning on the altars of their hearts the flame that is tortured out of ours.[32]

Solzhenitsyn's *Gulag Archipelago* itself suggests that, for some, the Gulag could be the desert in a much more searching way. For instance, when he speaks of the methods of interrogation used, he says:

> So what is the answer? How can you stand your ground when you are weak and sensitive to pain, when people you love are still alive, when you are unprepared?
>
> What do you need to make you stronger than the interrogator and the whole trap?
>
> From the moment you go to prison you must put your cosy past firmly behind you. At the very threshold, you must say to yourself: 'My life is over, a little early to be sure, but there's nothing to be done about it. I shall never return to freedom. I am condemned to die – now or a little later . . . For me those I love have died, and for them I have died . . .'
>
> Confronted by such a prisoner, the interrogation will tremble.
>
> Only the man who has renounced everything can win that victory.[33]

Throughout Solzhenitsyn's account of the Gulag, in which he is conscious that there is so much that he must simply put down for posterity, so that it is never forgotten: so much that there is hardly any chance to take breath, to analyse, to make anything of experiences that lay bare 'the rock bottom of a human being' and could provide material for endless novels[34] – throughout his account, remarks seem to pierce this relentless chronicle of human inhumanity that seem to come from another world, a world of privation and self-denial that felt itself on the threshold of paradise, the world of the Desert Fathers, of the Russian Forest. In the middle of his account of the institutionalized thieving of the transit convoys, Solzhenitsyn suddenly remarks: 'Own nothing! Possess nothing! Buddha and Christ taught us this, and the Stoics and the Cynics. Greedy though we are, why can't we seem to grasp that simple teaching? Can't we understand that with property we destroy our soul?'[35] Or again, speaking of the way in which, however humiliated, one seemed to leap at the opportunity to have some kind of position, however menial, some sense of control over one's destiny, however illusory, Solzhenitsyn comments:

> Submissiveness to fate, the total abdication of your own will in the shaping of your life, the recognition that it was impossible to guess the best and the worst ahead of time but that it was easy to take a step you would reproach yourself for – all this freed the prisoner from any bondage, made him calmer, and even ennobled him.[36]

None of this alters the fact that the inhumanity of the Gulag destroyed people, and crippled them emotionally and spiritually, as well as physically. But it does show that, as the Gulag reduced human beings to the 'rock bottom', in some it revealed a place 'beyond despair', revealed a humanity reborn beyond death. For some it could be a desert that became the threshold of paradise, and the lessons discovered by those who perceived this were the lessons of those who voluntarily sought the desert as a place where God could be found, or – perhaps nearer the mark so far as experience is concerned – of those who learnt to endure the desert of inner desolation and draw from that experience spiritual fruits they could transmit to others.

NOTES

For an account of Russian spirituality, see G. P. Fedotov, *The Russian Religious Mind*, 2 vols (Cambridge, Mass., 1946–66) and his anthology of translated sources, *A Treasury of Russian Spirituality* (London, 1950). For a briefer, though more critical and up-to-date account, see Fr Sergei Hackel's contributions to *Christian Spirituality*, vol. 2, ed. Jill Raitt, B. McGinn and J. Meyendorff (London, 1987), pp. 223–35, and vol. 3, ed. L. Dupré and D. E. Saliers (London, 1990), pp. 458–69; and *The Study of Spirituality*, ed. C. Jones, G. Wainwright and E. Yarnold SJ (London, 1986), pp. 259–76, and his bibliographies.

1   See Valentine Zander, *The Life of St Seraphim* (London, 1968), p. 7, n.3.
2   *The Russian Religious Mind*, vol. 2, pp. 195 f.
3   *Paterik* 7; in *The Paterik of the Kievan Caves Monastery*, tr. Muriel Heppell (Harvard Library of Early Ukrainian Literature, English Translations, vol. 1, 1989), pp. 19 f.
4   See Muriel Heppell's introd. to the original publication of Archimandrite Lazarus Moore's tr. of the *Ladder* (London, 1959), esp. pp. 27 ff.
5   *The Paterik of the Kievan Caves Monastery*, pp. 1–li.
6   *The Russian Religious Mind*, vol. 2, p. 221.
7   ibid. pp. 221 f. And see also J. Meyendorff, *Byzantium and the Rise of Russia* (Cambridge, 1981), esp. pp. 132–8.
8   For Paissy, see S. Chetverikov, *Starets Paisii Velichkovskii* (Eng. tr., Belmont, Mass., 1980).
9   Chetverikov, p. 124.
10 An English translation of the original Greek *Philokalia* is in progress, by G. E. H. Palmer, P. Sherrard and K. T. Ware (3 vols so far, London, 1979 ff); selections from St Theopan the Recluse's nineteenth-century Russian tr. of the *Philokalia* have been tr. into English by E. Kadloubovsky and G. E. H. Palmer (2 vols, London, 1951, 1954).
11 For Tikhon, see Nadejda Gorodetsky, *St Tikhon: inspirer of Dostoevsky* (London, 1951).
12 In *A Treasury of Russian Spirituality*, p. 191.
13 Gorodetsky, p. 19.
14 Quoted in ibid. p. 157.
15 ibid. p. 49.
16 ibid. pp. 72 f.
17 ibid. p. 158.

18 ibid. p. 161.
19 ibid. pp. 162 f. For a rather less rapturous attitude to the Russian spring, see Pushkin's poem 'Autumn', stanza 2, in, e.g., *The Penguin Book of Russian Verse*, ed. D. Obolensky (Harmondsworth, 1962), p. 106.
20 Gorodetsky, p. 153.
21 ibid. pp. 153 f.
22 For Seraphim, see Valentine Zander, *St Seraphim of Sarov* (Eng. tr., London, 1975).
23 See Zander, p. 19.
24 ibid.
25 ibid. p. 17.
26 Quoted in Hackel, *The Study of Spirituality*, p. 270.
27 For Amvrosy, see J. Dunlop, *Staretz Amvrosy: model for Dostoevsky's Staretz Zossima* (London, 1975).
28 Dunlop, p. 14.
29 Quoted in ibid. pp. 107 f.
30 ibid. p. 161.
31 Iulia de Beausobre, *A Flame in the Snow* (London, 1945), p. 8.
32 Quoted in Constance Babington Smith, *Iulia de Beausobre* (London, 1983), pp. 40 f.
33 A. Solzhenitsyn, *Gulag Archipelago*, vol. 1 (London, 1974) p. 130.
34 See Solzhenitsyn's remarks, ibid. p. 541.
35 ibid. p. 516.
36 ibid. p. 560.

8

The Waste Land and Beyond: T. S. Eliot

In his most influential poem, 'The Waste Land', T. S. Eliot used the imagery of pointlessness and lack of consequence to capture the nature of a city representing a civilization that had in the Great War come close to the brink of destruction. Although Eliot himself disclaimed such an interpretation of the poem as 'criticism of the contemporary world . . . [or] as an important piece of social criticism' and said that for him 'it was only the relief of a personal and wholly insignificant grouse against life; it is just a piece of rhythmical grumbling',[1] his poem was *heard* by many others as expressing something more than purely personal, as capturing a sense of desolation and meaninglessness – and more, in doing that, in finding words to articulate a mood, as pointing beyond the 'Waste Land'. Auden put it thus in a verse tribute:

> it was you
> Who, not speechless with shock but finding the right
> Language for thirst and fear, did most to
> Prevent a panic.[2]

In the same celebratory volume, Kathleen Raine said:

> In the 'etherized' sky, the humming street-lamp watching through the night hours, the pathos of the London crowd expressed once and for all in the allusive line, 'I had not thought death had undone so many'; the river carrying its memories past modern gas-works; in the very name, 'the Waste Land,' we recognized, as he created the images, the world of our own experience. Eliot, we recognized, was

the poet who had taken upon himself the burden of experiencing the world for his generation, as kings were formerly supposed to act and suffer for their tribes. It is in the nature of the poet's vocation that he should thus take upon himself the imaginative burden of his tribe. But it is not every poet who has taken it upon himself to experience and transmute such a great weight of human life and suffering; or who has found himself compelled to be the prophet of truths so terrible.[3]

Both W. H. Auden and Kathleen Raine claim that Eliot's creating the images that summoned up the pain and oppression of the 'Waste Land' did more than depict: for Auden, the very finding of language achieved something, prevented a 'panic'; for Raine, the poetic vocation is one of 'substitution and exchange' that bears its own fruit.

But in the poem itself, in its structure, Eliot seems to me to suggest another kind of resolution. In the notes to 'The Waste Land' he remarks in connection with the quotations from St Augustine's *Confessions* and the Buddha's Fire Sermon at the end of Part III (ll.307–11), that 'the collocation of these two representatives of eastern and western asceticism, as the culmination of this part of the poem, is not an accident.' The poem seems to be reaching out, by way of these two representatives of asceticism, to some sort of conclusion. Though Augustine himself could only with difficulty be regarded as a desert saint (his own pondering of a flight into the desert he represents as countered by God himself: see *Confessions* X.43.70), as a *representative* of western asceticism, he cannot but recall the Christian asceticism of the desert; while the Buddha was led from his father's palace to the forests and wastelands of North India, and so is the very epitome of a forest ascetic. So it might be said that a situation analysed in terms of the desert is directed towards the desert, the desert sought out by holy men and ascetics, for some remedy, some resolution, some meaning.

Similarly in the final section, 'What the Thunder said', Eliot turns to one of the Hindu Upanishads, the *Brihad-Aranyaka Upanishad*, for the Sanskrit words – *datta, dayadhvam, damyata*, and *shantih* (give, sympathize, control, peace) – in which the thunder answers, and with which the poem ends. The second part of the title of the Upanishad – Aranyaka – means forest, and Eliot included the word in a draft of the closing lines of 'East Coker' (but later deleted it). Helen Gardner comments:

> the Aranyakas are sacred books whose name can be interpreted as meaning either that they were written in the forest by forest hermits, or that they were written for those who, after a life of action, had retired to the forests . . . The forest is to eastern asceticism what the desert is to western.[4]

So the final part of 'The Waste Land' closes with words from the forest – or the desert. One of the earliest reviews of 'The Waste Land' complained about Eliot's use of these Sanskrit words:

> Why, again, Datta, Dayadhvam, Damyata? Or Shantih? Do they not say a good deal less for us than 'Give: sympathize: control' or 'Peace'? Of course; but Mr Eliot replies that he wants them not merely to mean those particular things, but also to mean them in a particular way – that is, to be remembered in connection with a Upanishad. Unfortunately, we have none of us this memory, nor can he give it to us . . . [5]

Maybe not, but if we know that they are Sanskrit words from an Upanishad, we know that that is where we are to look for the meaning they can offer, we know that it is to the forest, or the desert, that we are being directed.

It seems to me that the desert remained a source of inspiration and a place of meaning for Eliot: in his poems and in his plays, especially in the first three of his plays and in *Four Quartets*, Eliot turns to the desert and the spirituality of the desert – or the forest – for some kind of resolution.

Eliot's first three plays are all, in different ways, about the nature of sanctity (or, at least, in all of them this is an important theme). *Murder in the Cathedral* is directly about the sanctity of Thomas à Becket: the tempters all suggest ways in which Thomas might achieve something for himself; the

145

last tempter – the 'unexpected' one, but the only one whose suggestions seriously tempt Thomas – suggests that Thomas make martyrdom itself an achievement, his way to an enduring glory. The resolve to genuine sanctity – which in this case differs not at all so far as the action is concerned, but only in the intention behind the action – is expressed in the sermon Thomas preaches in the cathedral at Canterbury on Christmas Day:

> A Christian martyrdom is never an accident, for Saints are not made by accident. Still less is a Christian martyrdom the effect of a man's will to become a Saint, as a man by willing and contriving may become a ruler of men. A martyrdom is always the design of God, for His love of men, to warn them and to lead them, to bring them back to His ways. It is never the design of man; for the true martyr is he who has become the instrument of God, who has lost his will in the will of God, and who no longer desires anything for himself, not even the glory of being a martyr.[6]

Thomas' struggle with the tempters – with himself – is a struggle in which is reflected in his own soul the high politics of the age in which he lived, the attempt to reform the Church of entanglement with the world by asserting the Church's independence of human kingdoms, by insisting on the unworldliness of her priests through upholding celibacy and stamping out simony. But Thomas' struggle is also set, in the play, against the muddle and compromise of daily life – 'oppression and luxury . . . poverty and licence . . . minor injustice' – 'living and partly living' – expressed by the chorus of the women of Canterbury. This 'humble and tarnished frame of existence' is set against the martyrdom of Thomas, the making of a saint. Yet it is also suggested that the life of the saint, though in contrast with the 'living and partly living' of ordinary life, *through* that contrast opens up another possibility, another dimension, within and for ordinary life. So at the end of the play, the chorus adds to its praise and thanksgiving for all that God has given through creation, thanksgiving:

. . . for Thy mercies of blood, for Thy redemption by
        blood. For the blood of Thy martyrs and saints
Shall enrich the earth, shall create the holy places.
For wherever a saint has dwelt, wherever a martyr has given
        his blood for the blood of Christ,
There is holy ground, and the sanctity shall not depart
        from it
Though armies trample over it, though sightseers come with
        guide-books looking over it;
From where the western seas gnaw at the coast of Iona,
To the death in the desert, the prayer in forgotten places by
        the broken imperial column,
From such ground springs that which forever renews the
        earth
Though it is forever denied.[7]

The 'death in the desert' is too abrupt to be confidently
identified in this context, but from the way the same theme
is used in the next two plays it seems most likely that Eliot
is referring to the death in the desert of Charles de Foucauld.
Eliot knew about Foucauld's life from the biography by René
Bazin which was published in 1921. In a wireless talk given
during the Second World War, 'Towards a Christian Britain',
Eliot referred to Bazin's biography which conveyed the extraordinary 'spiritual quality' of Charles de Foucauld's life.[8] It
would seem very likely that he had read Bazin's book by the
time he wrote *Murder in the Cathedral*, and though in almost
every respect the lives of Charles de Foucauld and Thomas
à Becket were quite different, so far as their deaths *as martyrdom* are concerned there is ambiguity in each case. The ambiguity about Becket's death as martyrdom is that spelt out in
the play; the ambiguity about Charles de Foucauld's death
arises from the fact that the suspicion on the part of some of
the Tuaregs that he was a French spy was not altogether
without foundation.[9] In both cases it is on the *intention*, of
which we can never be entirely sure, that the question as to
whether this is a martyr's death turns.

In *The Family Reunion* the imagery of the desert is used both
to express the darkness and lack of communication of the
ordinary life of 'living and partly living' and to express the

way of 'sanctity' that leads beyond it. Before he makes his decision, Harry's own condition, both hard to be clear about in itself (did he kill his wife? or want to? or what?) and yet not sharply different from 'ordinary' life, is expressed in images that revolve round that of the desert:

> The sudden solitude in a crowded desert
> In a thick smoke, many creatures moving
> Without direction, for no direction
> Leads anywhere but round and round in that vapour –
> . . . One thinks to escape
> By violence, but one is still alone
> In an over-crowded desert, jostled by ghosts.[10]

Or later:

> In and out, in an endless drift
> Of shrieking forms in a circular desert
> Weaving with contagion of putrescent embraces
> On dissolving bone. In and out, the movement
> Until the chain broke, and I was left
> Under the single eye above the desert.[11]

But *where* Harry is going, when he makes his decision, is expressed in a passage that recalls the details of Charles de Foucauld's life as described by René Bazin:

> Somewhere on the other side of despair.
> To the worship in the desert, the thirst and deprivation,
> A stray sanctuary and a primitive altar,
> The heat of the sun and the icy vigil,
> A care over lives of humble people,
> The lesson of ignorance, of incurable diseases.
> Such things are possible. It is love and terror
> Of what waits and wants me, and will not let me fall.[12]

'On the other side of despair': that is where the life of sanctity calls.

The contrast between ordinary life and the life of the saint is worked out in more explicit terms in *The Cocktail Party* in

Sir Henry Harcourt-Reilly's talk to Celia Coplestone in his
consulting room. The ordinary life, the 'human condition',
maintained by 'the common routine' is lived by those who:

> Learn to avoid excessive expectation,
> Because tolerant of themselves and others,
> Giving and taking, in the usual actions
> What there is to give and take. They do not repine;
> Are contented with the morning that separates
> And with the evening that brings together
> For casual talk before the fire
> Two people who know they do not understand each other,
> Breeding children whom they do not understand
> And who will never understand them.[13]

This is Harry's being 'alone In an over-crowded desert,
jostled by ghosts'. But Harcourt-Reilly says, and should be
taken as meaning it: 'It is a good life. Though you will not
know how good Till you come to the end . . . In a world of
lunacy, Violence, stupidity, greed . . . it is a good life.'

The other life is not so easy to describe: we are not familiar
with it and so cannot describe it in familiar terms:

> The second is unknown, and so requires faith –
> The kind of faith that issues from despair.
> The destination cannot be described;
> You will know very little till you get there;
> You will journey blind. But the way leads towards
>   possession
> Of what you have sought for in the wrong place.[14]

This second way – like Harry's, beyond despair – is what
Celia chooses, though she fears it will be a lonely way, to
which comes the reply:

> No lonelier than the other. But those who take the other
> Can forget their loneliness. You will not forget yours.
> Each way means loneliness – and communion.

Both ways avoid the final desolation
Of solitude in the phantasmal world
Of imagination, shuffling memories and desires.[15]

What Eliot is presenting here, through the mouth of Harcourt-Reilly, is the traditional Christian doctrine of the Two
Ways, hinted at in passages like Matthew 19:21 and 12, and
developed from the fourth century onwards. The ordinary
Christian life, of faithful fulfilment of duties and a life of
virtue, is one life: it is 'living and partly living', there is little
heroic about it, but it is a good life, and in a fallen world that
is no mean thing. The other life is the life of the 'saint', it
involves renunciation of earthly loves including marriage, so
as to make possible a single-minded love of God. Both lives
are good, neither life is 'better'; but ordinary life runs a risk
– the risk of seeking in human love what can only be given
by divine love. Part of the point of the life of the saint is to
remind one that what love seeks cannot be satisfied by human
love. Geoffrey Faber found Eliot's account of marriage and
family life untrue to experience; Eliot's reply insisted that in
the 'universe of discourse' of Harcourt-Reilly's speech 'there
are two primary propositions: 1. nobody understands you but
God, 2. all real love is ultimately the love of God'.[16]

Although Eliot's view of ordinary human relationships *is*
sombre, it expresses an insight, or a conviction, not at all
uncommon in the Christian tradition. St Augustine too had
a deep sense of human loneliness: 'in the sojourning of this
fleshly life each one carries his own heart, and every heart is
closed to every other heart'.[17] We long to overcome this loneliness, but to think that any kind of human communion that
it is in our power to create – even the companionship of
marriage – can *overcome* this fundamental loneliness, rather
than assuage it, is to underestimate the darkness that has
fallen between us as a result of the Fall. This is not, however,
an insight confined to believers. In a letter the poet Rilke
expressed some impatience with those who ask of married
people if they are happy, with the implication that they ought
to be – no one would ever expect that of someone single!
Rilke went on:

Togetherness [*Miteinander*] between two human beings is an impossibility and, when it seems to occur, a limitation, a mutual compromise, which robs one side, or both, of their fullest freedom and development. But, once the awareness is granted, that even between the *closest* of human beings there remains an infinite distance, then a wonderful living-alongside-each-other [*Nebeneinanderwohnen*] can spring up, when they succeed in loving the distance between them, something that makes it possible for them to see each other in their wholeness and against the background of the vastness of heaven![18]

Eliot dwells more on the frustration and disillusion of human companionship, which may owe something to his own experience of his first marriage, and his perception of his parents' relationship (that they were both lonely people, together with his sense of not living up to his father's expectations of him).[19] Rilke points rather to how this sense of aloneness can lead to a sense of difference and wonder. For Eliot, that sense of difference was perhaps disclosed by the contrast with the life of the saint: it is more uncompromisingly something given, something the other side of despair.

But to return to *The Cocktail Party*: Celia becomes a missionary, goes to Africa, and suffers death by crucifixion 'very near an ant-hill'. It seems clear that Eliot's vision of Celia's vocation is inspired by Charles de Foucauld, especially as Harcourt-Reilly, trying to explain something of Celia's vocation to suffer, refers to the 'Saint in the desert'.[20] Celia's friends, learning about her death at another cocktail party, exclaim about the 'waste' of her life.

Eliot, in his attempts to explore something of the nature of sanctity in his first three plays, returned again and again to the image of Charles de Foucauld. Why? One reason Eliot himself seems to give in the wireless talk already referred to. Charles de Foucauld's aim 'was not primarily to convert by teaching, but to *live* the Christian life, alone among the natives'.[21] Argument and propaganda meant little for Eliot (his own faith embraced a profound scepticism), what carries conviction is the quality of a life. The other reason why Eliot returned to the image of Foucauld is perhaps that the way of

the desert speaks in uncompromising terms: the sense that
extreme remedies are necessary to cut through the indifference
(as much moral as intellectual) that Christianity faces in the
twentieth century. Eliot was convinced that

> through the mysterious power of holiness, which is the
> power of God, [Charles de Foucauld] achieved something
> for the world which should make us feel very modest about
> all our schemes and plans. I think that it is through such
> men as Foucauld that the reborn Christian consciousness
> comes; and I think that from the point of view which we
> should take, there is no higher glory of a Christian empire
> than that which was brought into being by a death in the
> desert.

Anyone familiar with *Four Quartets* will have been reminded
time and again during the preceding paragraphs of phrases
and images from these poems: 'an occupation for a saint –
No occupation either, but something given . . .', 'A condition
of complete simplicity (Costing not less than everything)'; or:
'A dignified and commodious sacrament' celebrated by 'the
music Of the weak pipe and the little drum'. That is hardly
surprising: *Four Quartets* (1936–42) was published between
Murder in the Cathedral (1935) and *The Cocktail Party* (1949).
Eliot himself said that 'Burnt Norton' was written from 'bits
left over from *Murder in the Cathedral*',[22] and in *The Family
Reunion* and even in *The Cocktail Party* one can detect (as one
does not in the later plays) reverberations from the verse of
Four Quartets. In a way, themes are discussed in his first three
plays (there is a deal of discussion) in a dramatic medium
that T. S. Eliot never seems to have quite made his own, that
are drawn together in a much more compelling way in *Four
Quartets*. It might seem that here the desert theme is set aside.
The reference to 'Aranyaka, the forest' at the end of 'East
Coker' was, as we have seen, dropped, so that 'a further
union, a deeper communion' is sought

> Through the dark cold and the empty desolation
> The wave cry, the wind cry, the vast waters
> Of the petrel and the porpoise . . .

There is an explicit reference to the desert in Part I of 'Little Gidding':

> There are other places
> Which also are the world's end, some at the sea jaws,
> Or over a dark lake, in a desert or a city . . .

The reference to the 'desert' seems to have floated in and out of the drafts, but Eliot gave his own identification of the places which 'also are at the world's end': the 'sea jaws' spoke of Iona and St Columba and of Lindisfarne and St Cuthbert; the 'dark lake' of the lake of Glendalough and St Kevin's hermitage in County Wicklow; the 'desert' of the hermits of the Thebaid and St Antony; the 'city' of Padua and the other St Antony.[23] Almost all the places 'at the world's end' recall the tradition that began, as we have seen, in the Egyptian desert and shaped the ascetic tradition of Christendom. The community that Nicholas Ferrar gathered around himself in the early seventeenth century at Little Gidding also drew on that tradition with the emphasis in its spiritual discipline on the Psalms and on the night as a time for prayer.

It seems to me, however, that the way in which the desert is appealed to as a source of meaning and resolution in 'The Waste Land' (through the collocation of two representatives of eastern and western asceticism, and the use of Sanskrit words from an Upanishad) and in the exploration of sanctity in his first three plays (through the evocation of Foucauld's 'death in the desert') is also found in *Four Quartets*. It comes to the surface in the long quotation from St John of the Cross in 'East Coker', the reference to the *Bhagavad-Gita* in 'The Dry Salvages', and in the repeated quotations from Julian of Norwich (supplemented by a phrase from *The Cloud of Unknowing*) in 'Little Gidding'. Earlier chapters in this book have suggested how St John of the Cross and Julian of Norwich can be regarded as belonging to the desert tradition of Christian spirituality; our discussion earlier in this chapter of 'Aranyaka – the forest' in connection with Hindu literature would seem to draw the *Bhagavad-Gita* into the parallel 'forest' tradition of Indian mysticism. It remains to suggest how this appeal to elements of the desert or forest tradition becomes a kind of well of meaning for *Four Quartets*. (To do this is to do no more than trace one strand in the complex tapestry of *Four Quartets*: there is nothing exhaustive or exclusive about what follows.)

The quotation from St John of the Cross comes as the poet responds to his reader's sense that there is repetition of what has been said before. He says he will say it again, and what he says is:

> . . . In order to arrive there
> To arrive where you are, to get from where you are not,
>   You must go by a way wherein there is no ecstasy.
> In order to arrive at what you do not know
>   You must go by a way which is the way of ignorance.
> In order to possess what you do not possess
>   You must go by the way of dispossession.
> In order to arrive at what you are not
>   You must go through the way in which you are not.
> And what you do not know is the only thing you know
> And what you own is what you do not own
> And where you are is where you are not.[24]

They are a fairly close translation (though not very close, so far as I can ascertain, to any existing English translation) of lines quoted above in the chapter on St John of the Cross: lines that occur in the *Ascent of Mount Carmel*, both in the body of the work, and inscribed at the foot of the sketch of Mount Carmel that prefaces that work.[25] They spell out the rationale of the direct ascent of the Mount – the way of perfect spirit – and mark it off uncompromisingly from the 'ways of imperfect spirit', ways of attachment, whether to temporal or spiritual things. They recall the distinction between the 'two lives' that Eliot appeals to in his plays: the life of ordinary virtue and the life of heroic sanctity. This distinction, or contrast, is in some ways softened, in some ways accentuated: softened in that Eliot sounds more tolerant, less sombre, in his picture of marriage at the beginning of 'East Coker' compared with what we have seen in his (later) *The Cocktail Party*, but accentuated in that what humans can *achieve* seems reduced to vanishing point – 'Do not let me hear Of the wisdom of old men . . . their folly, Their fear':

> The only wisdom we can hope to acquire
> Is the wisdom of humility: humility is endless.[26]

Even faith, hope and love are not virtues we could cultivate: what we can do in respect of them is more like letting go of them: and that is what is said again in the lines Eliot borrows from St John of the Cross.

'A way wherein there is no ecstasy.' Earlier, in 'The Waste Land' Eliot had prized ecstasy:

> *Datta*: what have we given?
> My friend, blood shaking my heart
> The awful daring of a moment's surrender
> Which an age of prudence can never retract
> By this, and this only, we have existed
> Which is not to be found in our obituaries . . .[27]

Not that Eliot exactly retracts this, but he revalues ecstasy and seeks more than a *moment's* surrender, though it is still surrender, not any kind of achievement such as an obituary might record, that holds the key:

> . . . echoed ecstasy
> Not lost, but requiring, pointing to the agony
> Of death and birth.[28]

Not merely something not retracted in the past, but something whose echoes reach into the future. So Eliot turns from 'the intense moment Isolated' to 'a lifetime's burning in every moment', which in 'The Dry Salvages' he sees as

> . . . something given
> And taken, in a lifetime's death in love,
> Ardour and selflessness and self-surrender.

That is for the saint:

> For most of us, there is only the unattended
> Moment, the moment in and out of time,
> The distraction fit, lost in a shaft of sunlight . . .[29]

And yet the life of the saint gives shape and direction to our lives: the moment of surrender gives a glimpse of the nature of love, not some emotion or preference, something that needs testing and purifying – in that 'lifetime's death in love' that is the occupation of the saint.

In 'The Dry Salvages', it is Krishna's admonishment of Arjuna 'on the field of battle' that articulates the spirituality of the forest. Krishna speaks to Arjuna about the purity of intention that justifies the action. It is not a matter of calculation and achievement: the hoped-for ends do not justify the means. 'And do not think of the fruit of action. Fare forward': 'For us, there is only the trying, The rest is not our business' (as Eliot has already put it in 'East Coker'). The intention that made Thomas' death at Canterbury martyrdom rather than a calculated striving after glory: concern for intention, a readiness, an ability to let go – 'that is the one action . . . Which shall fructify in the lives of others'.

Quotations from Julian of Norwich and *The Cloud of Unknowing* (exact quotations this time, so exact that one can verify which editions Eliot had recourse to)[30] draw 'Little Gidding' to its close. Though Helen Gardner in her indispensable book, *The Composition of Four Quartets*, somewhat plays down the importance of knowing where Eliot's quotations come from in *Four Quartets*,[31] it seems to me that something *is* lost if the echoes of Julian and the *Cloud* are not picked up. At the very least, the *titles* of these works are important: Julian's *Revelations of Divine Love* (as Eliot would have known it) and *The Cloud of Unknowing*, the former declaring that what Julian heard and sets forth manifests the *love* of God, and the latter speaking of that dimension of Christian life and belief that transcends human comprehension, so that the apophatic (to use the technical term for the theology of negations, where we express our sense of God by denying the adequacy of any human concepts) makes space for the sceptical and the questing.

The doctrine of the two lives also makes a final appearance, but in a much-transformed guise:

> There are three conditions which often look alike
> Yet differ completely, flourish in the same hedgerow:
> Attachment to self and to things and to persons, detachment
> From self and from things and from persons; and, growing between them, indifference
> Which resembles the others as death resembles life,
> Being between two lives – unflowering, between
> The live and the dead nettle.[32]

The way of attachment and the way of detachment are the two lives: the life of ordinary virtue, expressed in attachment to, and care for, people and things and places, and the life of heroic sanctity, or radical detachment. But *both* are now valued, both are 'life' – in contrast to indifference, which is death. (It does not seem to me that the live and dead nettle are being contrasted – rather than compared – with each other: after all it is the unpromisingly named dead nettle that is the more beautiful.) One wonders if the doctrine of the two lives (in which, traditionally, one life was valued above the other, despite the kind of disclaimers Eliot puts into Harcourt-Reilly's mouth) has not been assimilated to the notion of the two *ways*, the way of affirmation and the way of negation; and Charles Williams' advocacy of their truly equal and complementary value heeded by Eliot.[33]

Attachment to finite beings is inevitably partial, which can lead to conflict and antagonism. But the balance of the two ways – of attachment and of detachment, which never leads to indifference – allows 'faces and places... To become renewed, transfigured, in another pattern', just as happiness for Harry in *The Family Reunion*:

> Did not consist in getting what one wanted
> Or in getting rid of what can't be got rid of
> But in a different vision.[34]

That mention of renewal, transfiguration, occasions the first evocation of Julian:

> Sin is Behovely, but
> All shall be well, and
> All manner of thing shall be well.

These are dangerous words: they run the risk of sounding complacent and merely optimistic. The risk is avoided by Julian herself because the words grow out of her perception of the overwhelming reality of the love of God: they are not cheap words, easily uttered, but words mined from the precious ore of her experience. But the poet is not the saint: as Hermann Broch remarks in connection with Virgil, 'he hears the call beyond the border, and all he may do is to capture it in the poem but not to follow it, paralysed by the injunction and bound to the spot, a scrivener this side of the border . . .'[35] The poet has to stay where he is, and find poetic means to avoid betraying the words of the saint who has heard the call and followed beyond the border, beyond despair. Christopher Ricks identifies the poetic means Eliot uses here in the line endings in *but* and *and* (that Eliot had used in his earlier poetry in quite a different way): 'the quotation from Dame Julian of Norwich is saved from complacency by the tentativeness, the tremulousness even (though within this sheer faith), in the *but* and the *and* at the ends of the lines'.[36] In this way Eliot captures in his poetry the faith that informed Julian's life, a faith that discovers a confidence, not in anything particular, not by overlooking 'things ill done and done to others' harm Which once you took for exercise of virtue', but in the purposes of that love named

> Behind the hands that wove
> The intolerable shirt of flame
> Which human power cannot remove.

The final triumph of that love, expressed in Julian's words 'And all shall be well and All manner of thing shall be well' is achieved by means, expressed in a couplet that combines a summary of Krishna's teaching with a phrase from Julian

– another striking collocation of representatives of eastern and western asceticism:

> By the purification of the motive
> In the ground of our beseeching.[37]

For Julian, the 'ground of our beseeching' is Christ himself, which is why it/we cannot fail, and why the 'purification of the motive' exacts a conformity to the life, death and resurrection of Christ: 'Hard and bitter agony for us, like Death, our death'.[38]

'With the drawing of this Love and the voice of this Calling': it is only in *response* to that that we can stir ourselves and turn to God and enter into the cloud of unknowing where 'thou mayest neither see him clearly by the light of understanding in thy reason, or feel him in sweetness of love in thine affection'.[39] The poem closes by drawing, as it were, from beyond itself towards:

> A condition of complete simplicity
> (Costing not less than everything)
> And all shall be well and
> All manner of thing shall be well
> When the tongues of flame are in-folded
> Into the crowned knot of fire
> And the fire and the rose are one.[40]

NOTES

1 *The Waste Land. A facsimile and transcript . . .* , ed. Valerie Eliot (London, 1971), p. 1.
2 *T. S. Eliot: a symposium*, ed. Tambimuttu and Richard March (London, 1948), p. 43.
3 ibid. pp. 78 f.
4 Helen Gardner, *The Composition of Four Quartets* (London, 1978), p. 113.
5 Review by Conrad Aiken, repr. in *T. S. Eliot: the man and his work*, ed. Allen Tate (London, 1967), p. 199.
6 *The Complete Plays of T. S. Eliot* (London, 1962), p. 33.

7   ibid. pp. 53 f.

8   'Towards a Christian Britain' in *The Listener* 25 (January-June 1941), pp. 524 f; referred to in Lyndall Gordon, *Eliot's New Life* (Oxford, 1988), p. 318.

9   See above, pp. 12 f.

10 *Complete Plays*, p. 66.

11 ibid. p. 107.

12 ibid. p. 111.

13 ibid. p. 189.

14 ibid. p. 190.

15 ibid. pp. 190 f.

16 See Lyndall Gordon, pp. 176 f.

17 Augustine, *Enarrationes in Psalmos* 55.9.

18 Letter to Emanuel von Bodman (17.vii.1901) in R. M. Rilke, *Briefe* (Wiesbaden, 1950), pp. 27–9.

19 See his letter to his brother after his father's death: *Letters of T. S. Eliot*, vol. 1 (1988), p. 273.

20 Lyndall Gordon, p. 175, supports such an interpretation.

21 See above, note 8.

22 Quoted in Helen Gardner, p. 39.

23 ibid. p. 163.

24 *Complete Poems 1909–1962* (London, 1963), p. 201.

25 See above, p. 92.

26 *Complete Poems*, p. 199.

27 ibid. pp. 78 f.

28 ibid. p. 201.

29 ibid. pp. 212 f.

30 Hugh Paulinus (in religion: Serenus) Cressy's tr. of Julian (1670): *XVI Revelations of Divine Love shewed to Mother Juliana of Norwich* (repr., e.g., with an introd. by G. Tyrrell, London 1902); Dom Justin McCann's edition of *The Cloud of Unknowing* (Orchard Books, 4; London, 1924).

31 Helen Gardner, p. 30.

32 *Complete Poems*, p. 219.

33 See esp. Charles Williams' study of Dante, *The Figure of Beatrice* (London, 1943) and also his essays in *The Image of the City*, ed. Anne Ridler (Oxford, 1958), Section V, pp. 147–68.

34 *Complete Plays*, p. 106.

35 Hermann Broch, *The Death of Virgil* (Eng. tr., 1946; repr. 1977), p. 137.

36 Christopher Ricks, *T. S. Eliot and Prejudice* (London, 1988), p. 258.

37 *Complete Poems*, p. 220.

38 From 'Journey of the Magi', in ibid. p. 110.
39 *Cloud of Unknowing*, ch. 3 (McCann, ed. cit. p. 12). (The quotation in the poem is from ch. 2, ed. cit. p. 9.)
40 *Complete Poems*, pp. 222 f.

Index

Thomas, K. 108
Tikhon 126, 129–33, 135, 136
Tolstoy, L. 136
Traherne, T. 94
Trinity, Holy 79

Varsanuphios 58
Vega, Lope de 88
Victoria, T. L. de 88

Visitation of BVM 11
Vladimir 123
Virgil 158

Walls, R. 56f
Wesley, J. 116
Williams, C. 109, 157
Worde, W. de 64